FRIDAYS

WITH

TRISTAN

UNDERSTANDING ADHD FROM A MENTORING PERSPECTIVE

Fridays With Tristan
First published September 2018 by Black Jack Books

©Grace da Camara
SafeZone Counselling
szcounselling@gmail.com

Illustrations by Ams Douse

Foreword by Dr Madalena Bennett MBCHB, FRACGP, DCB

ISBN 978-0-9944802-5-5

Foreword

So, you've been told you have ADHD? What does that even mean? As if being a teen isn't hard enough!

Having ADHD may make you feel different, and it may even make you feel less smart than your peers, but it is important for you to know that you are not alone.

This book is written by an insightful and caring practitioner who works with young people with ADHD. Because of her personal experiences with this condition she has a special interest and is passionate about ADHD. In it, you'll meet 13-year-old Tristan with whom you may relate, as well as the 17-year-old Xavier, who (in a manner of speaking) 'has been there before'. He was diagnosed with ADHD when he was 13, and is now a 'Peer Helper' at his school. They share their experiences in a unique way.

As a general practitioner (GP), I have met many teens, along with their families, with experiences very similar to both Tristan and Xavier. Whether you are starting your ADHD journey and are still waiting to be diagnosed, or are already living with a diagnosis of ADHD, your family GP can be a valuable source of guidance and ongoing support.

Up till now your caregivers (parents, aunts, uncles, grandparents) have guided and protected you, and most of the time they have made many of your decisions. So, how can they continue to protect and guide you, through your transition into adulthood, with all its challenges, while also coping with your struggles with ADHD?

In this book, Grace will gently guide you on your ADHD journey, with Tristan in the midst of it all – angry, upset and feeling very alone. The kind and likeable Xavier, who has ADHD himself, becomes the 'Mentor' that Tristan needs and helps him dispel the thought that having ADHD means that you are 'stupid' and 'lazy'!

Throughout the book, Xavier helps Tristan understand ADHD; he supports Tristan as he prepares for a possible diagnosis of ADHD, helping him make sense of confusing information and myths around the condition. Xavier reminds Tristan that he is not alone, and that ADHD is all around.

 I would encourage you to not only take from this book all that you find helpful, but to also share the knowledge and advocate for yourself and others who are faced with similar challenges.

Perhaps you, too, could be someone's Xavier one day!

Dr Maddie

A big thank you to my children and grandchildren, you are my social laboratory, the source of my inspiration, and my world. To my husband, thank you for your selfless nature, and for supporting my every dream.

Contents

To the Reader:

The purpose of this guide is to provide you with information about ADHD and to share with you a peer mentoring view of living with ADHD.

The ultimate aim of this guide is for you to understand that having ADHD is nothing to be ashamed of or embarrassed about. It is not simply a nicer way of saying that someone is 'lazy' or 'stupid'. ADHD is a real condition, experienced by many, that is also manageable.

Everyone is unique, whether they have ADHD or any other diagnosis, or no diagnosis at all. Not everything in this book will apply to you, but you are sure to find something you will relate to. You may already have a diagnosis of ADHD, like Xavier, or you might be more like Tristan who is only just starting the process. Your family situation and personal history might be completely different from either Xavier or Tristan. But some of their experiences and challenges may be similar to what you're going through.

Mentoring, in this guide, refers to one person helping another through challenges. The mentor is usually older and has experienced challenges of their own, and uses their knowledge to assist the mentee. Assistance can be in the form of providing a listening ear, directions to counselling and other services, and sharing their own challenges. Mentors help mentees to overcome challenges, develop their talents, and find their way in the world.

The relationship relies on connection and trust. A mentor can be anyone from a family friend or teacher, to a professional mentor or counsellor, as long as the mentee feels supported and encouraged. Tristan happens to find Xavier, who has also experienced ADHD, but mentors do not have to have been through the exact same struggles as you. Anyone you feel comfortable with can play the role of mentor for you.

For all those who have ADHD, I hope that this book helps you to accept your diagnosis and to move forward, recognising that ADHD does not define you, and individuals from every walk of life share similar journeys and struggles.

Read and Be Empowered.

Grace

ADHD according to Xavier

What does having ADHD really mean to a Teen?

I want you to know that having ADHD doesn't have to get in the way of living the life you want. Many teens with ADHD have grown up to follow their passions, live happy lives, have families and be successful in their work. They've found this success because they've taken the time to learn how ADHD affects them, and they have taken charge of a treatment plan that works for them and their own situation.

My name is Xavier and I was diagnosed with Attention Deficit Hyperactivity Disorder (ADHD) the year that I started high school.

I often wondered, "Why me? Why did I have to be the one with ADHD?" I felt a sense of guilt, as if I had done something wrong. I have now learned that having ADHD is not my fault. Research has clearly shown that ADHD runs in families (due to genetics). ADHD is a brain-based disorder, and the symptoms shown in ADHD are linked to many specific brain areas. Although there is no known cure for ADHD, we know of many strategies that can reduce the impact that ADHD has on your everyday life.

A few months back I read the following simple explanation of how it feels to have ADHD. Imagine...

Four teens line up to race the 1000 metres. All of them wear shorts and sneakers, but the fourth one also carries a 25kg backpack. It should not surprise anyone that the fourth runner will most likely fall behind the others. Now, imagine the 25kg backpack is transparent – that is what it is like to have ADHD. I often felt ashamed, stigmatised, embarrassed and isolated, carrying this load.

I am that runner with the backpack and I know I may never outpace my peers, but I run anyway. Life requires it. I could have chosen to give up, but I chose to race, even knowing

1

that although I may not win, I would most definitely lose if I did not give it a try. Life is about choices. It is about choosing to live the best life that I can, despite having ADHD, or any other condition for that matter.

However, looking back there are several things I wish I had known when I was first diagnosed. Most importantly, *I wish somebody had told me ...*

You aren't 'Stupid' and you aren't 'Lazy'!

In my first year of high school, I was spending twice as many hours as my classmates to complete assignments, and my home life frequently felt like a battlefield. At times I felt pretty stupid and thought that I must be lazy, otherwise I would have done my schoolwork without my parents and teachers having to nag me. Struggling with schoolwork was probably the worst part of having ADHD. You see, I really wanted to do well to impress my parents (especially my dad who compared me with my very smart, younger brother). No matter how hard I tried, I just could not meet my dad's expectations.

I also wish that someone had told me why I had trouble concentrating. I learned later that sometimes when a student with ADHD is trying to listen to his parents or teachers, it's like trying to send an electrical current along a wire where there are some bad connections. Not all the messages can get through and your mind wanders. You may daydream, or get easily distracted. This gets you in trouble for 'not listening'.

When you have a condition like ADHD you don't know what 'normal' attention and concentration is. You assume that everyone concentrates the same way as you do. It's like having a vision impairment. You don't know what the real world looks like, until you're tested and get glasses.

Let's not forget the positives!

There is no question that living with ADHD has many challenges. Some of these challenges suck, but not all. Once you identify your positive traits, build your support system, and find out where you thrive, you can work towards putting your perceived shame behind you. Many of us have a wonderful zest for life and are tenacious – we keep trying, even when it is hard. We are resilient, kind and forgiving. Figure out your interests and strengths, and focus your efforts there. Embrace your

ADHD! Enjoy being the more emotional, forgetful, natural, funny, intuitive, inspirational, procrastinating, unplanned, passionate ADHD you. Avoid a life in which you try not to be ADHD. Rather, find one in which you can be ADHD, be yourself, do what comes naturally, do what you are passionate about and engaged by.

Once I embraced my ADHD, it became easier to cope with the challenges. Because I don't hide my ADHD, I do not feel shame in it.

I now take every opportunity to speak up and advocate for children with ADHD.

Good luck with your ADHD journey.

Xavier

Why Am I Different?

Many children with ADHD feel shame about being different from their peers. Teens feel this more acutely than adults. According to Dr Dodson (a psychiatrist specialising in adults with ADHD), for many people with ADHD shame arises from the repeated failure to meet expectations from parents, teachers, friends, and the world. Children desperately want to fit in with their friends, and dislike things that make them stand out or draw attention to themselves. Besides the behavioural differences that ADHD can bring (such as hyperactivity and impulsivity), there are other differences to having ADHD. For example, having doctors' appointments or extra help at school. ADHD affects everyone's behaviour differently, but feeling ashamed of it is a common theme in teens.

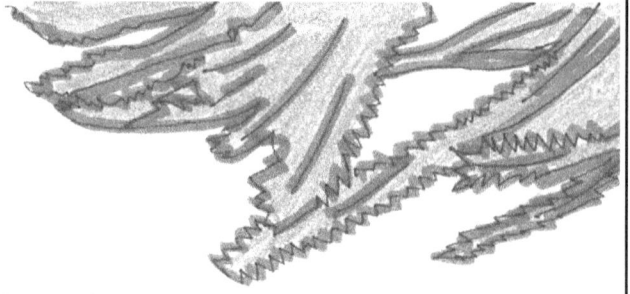

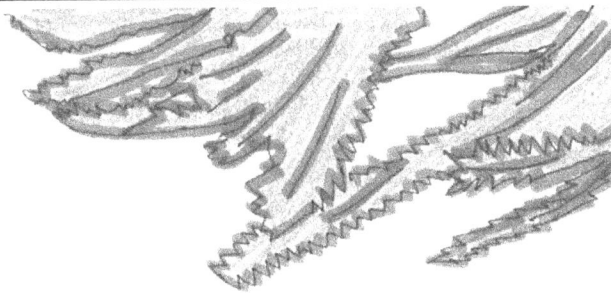

FACT: In Australia, the Child and Adolescent Component of the National Survey of Mental Health and Well-Being, reported ADHD to be present in 11% of children and adolescents (Sawyer et al, 2000). With this current prevalence, it is likely that there are children with ADHD in every school and educational facility, and that teachers interact with students with ADHD in many settings such as classrooms, playgrounds and sports grounds daily. It is important, therefore, that teachers have a sound understanding of the challenges that students with ADHD face. (Research to date suggests that although teachers have some knowledge about ADHD, there are gaps in their knowledge as well as some misconceptions.)

School creates multiple challenges for children with ADHD. The very tasks these students find the most difficult—sitting still, listening quietly, concentrating—are the ones they are required to do all day long. Perhaps most frustrating of all is that most these children want to be able to learn and behave like their unaffected peers. They do not want to stand out or be different. Neurological deficits, not unwillingness, keep kids with attention deficit disorder from learning in traditional ways.

Experts, like Dr William Dodson, a leading expert in adult ADHD, estimate that by the time a child with ADHD turns twelve, he/she will have received 20,000 more negative messages than his/her neurotypical peers. The daily struggle to prove their worth can make teens with ADHD question whether they have what it takes to make it in school, and beyond. This fear of falling short is more intense for individuals with ADHD.

Unfortunately, children with ADHD may be hassled by adults (including teachers and parents) for lack of effort. Some adults may even say things like, "You're lazy" and "You don't try hard enough". We know that these statements are not true, but they still make children feel bad about themselves.

ADHD acts as a magnifying glass, intensifying each challenge that a teen faces. Instead of dealing with the demands and pressures they face from parents and teachers, many adolescents deal with this stress in a different, less obvious way. They opt out of the competition altogether, and stop trying to do well at school (Price, A., 2017).

Children with ADHD are constantly corrected for their impulsivity, hyperactivity, or inattention. Over time, that criticism adds up and slowly undermines the child's self-esteem (the ability to cope with the basic challenges of life and being worthy of happiness), and confidence tank.

Researchers tell us that when adults with ADHD are asked how they coped, they often say, 'Someone believed in me.' That 'someone' was most often their parents, but the next most-often listed person was a teacher. A teacher who understands ADHD and learning disabilities can make a meaningful difference in children's lives. Become that inspiring teacher your students will remember into adulthood.

"If a child can't learn the way we teach, maybe we should teach the way they learn."

– Ignacio Estrada

Take Away: Succeeding in school is one of the most beneficial things that can happen to a child! Parents and teachers need to work together to help each child succeed in school and reach his/her full potential. Ask yourself the question: Are my expectations of my child/my student with ADHD realistic?

"

Everyone is a genius, but if you judge a fish by its ability to climb a tree, it will live its whole life believing that it is stupid.

— Albert Einstein

"

CHAPTER TWO

What is ADHD?

Tristan arrived promptly and seemed excited, but slightly apprehensive, about the meeting. He was especially curious about the name on the door and wanted to know what I did there.

Tris: So, what do you do here?

Xavier: I am a Peer Mentor, which means that I help kids who may be going through some tough times.

Tris: Lucky me for dropping my phone then?

Xavier: Well, I suppose you could say that! By the way do you remember that I told you that I knew a kid who was very much like the way you were describing yourself yesterday?

Tris: Yep, I do. Who is it?

Xavier: Well, that kid was me four years ago!

Tris: No way! Were you really a loser like me then?

Xavier: No, I was not so much a loser; I just found some things difficult and struggled to fit in. So, how was your day?

Tris: Well, today was a bad day for me. Actually, most days are! I got told off by Mrs Smart, struggled in English and had no one to hang around with during lunch. The whole day my mind has been going like the 'spin cycle' of a washing machine; so many thoughts rushing around in my head … and to top it all I now have to go and see some doctor. Mrs Smart told my mum that there's something wrong with me. She thinks I have ADHD – whatever that is!

Xavier: ADHD! That sucks. I have ADHD too.

Tris: Do you really have ADHD? I thought that I was the only one who had it in the whole school! Was it Mrs Smart who told you that you had ADHD?

Xavier: No, Mr Bighead told my parents that there was something wrong with my ability to concentrate; that I spoke out of turn, was disruptive and needed to work harder.

Tris: Really! If that's what ADHD is then I can't have ADHD. Mrs Smart told my mum that I daydream, don't complete tasks and that I'm easily distracted.

Xavier: Those are struggles common to ADHD as well; but just another type.

Tris: What do you mean by 'type'? And how do you know all this? I have a dog and his name is Amigo.

Xavier: Lucky you! I've always wanted a dog, but pets aren't allowed in our apartment.

I know about the different types of ADHD because I was diagnosed four years ago. I was told that I had the combined type, which means that I have symptoms of Inattention, Hyperactivity and Impulsivity.

Tris: If I have ADHD, will my doctor tell me what type I have?

Xavier: Doctors are all different. Some just say that you have ADHD and don't really explain. In my case, because I didn't really know much about ADHD back then, my mum did most of the talking and she asked Dr Cool which type I had. If you want, I can help you learn more about ADHD.

Tris: You would really do that for me?

Xavier: Of course, mate! What about we meet for the rest of the school term every Friday from 3:00 to 3:30?

Tris: That's cool with me! Same time next Friday then.

FACT: ADHD stands for Attention Deficit Hyperactivity Disorder. The term is used broadly to include all individuals with attention deficit, even those who are not hyperactive. *The Diagnostic and Statistical Manual of Mental Disorders (DSM- 5)*, lists three subtypes of ADHD:

- ADHD predominantly hyperactive and impulsive
- ADHD predominantly inattentive
- ADHD combined type

Typically, ADHD symptoms arise in early childhood. According to the *DSM-5*, several symptoms are required to be present before the age of twelve. In making the diagnosis, children up to sixteen need to have six or more symptoms of the disorder present; adolescents (seventeen and older) and adults should have at least five of the symptoms. Below is a summary of each subtype, adapted from the *DSM-5*

ADHD predominantly hyperactive-impulsive type

- Fidgets with hands or feet, or squirms in chair
- Has difficulty remaining seated
- Runs about or climbs excessively (in children); extreme restlessness (in adults)
- Difficulty engaging in activities quietly
- Acts as if driven by a motor
- Talks excessively
- Blurts out answers before questions have been completed
- Difficulty waiting or taking turns
- Interrupts or intrudes upon others

ADHD predominantly inattentive type

- Fails to give close attention to details or makes careless mistakes
- Has difficulty sustaining attention
- Does not appear to listen
- Struggles to follow through with instructions
- Has difficulty with being organised
- Avoids or dislikes tasks requiring sustained mental effort
- Loses things
- Is easily distracted
- Is forgetful in daily activities

ADHD combined type

- The individual meets the criteria for both inattention and hyperactive-impulsive ADHD presentations.

It is important to note that the above difficulties are not solely unique to people with ADHD. Many people without ADHD also have trouble at times with paying attention, listening, or waiting their turn. However, individuals with ADHD have trouble with these things almost all the time, leading to impairments in their functioning.

Severity of symptoms: ADHD symptoms affect each person to varying degrees. Clinicians can designate the severity of ADHD as 'mild', 'moderate' or 'severe' (*DSM-5*).

Mild: Few symptoms beyond the required number for diagnosis are present, and symptoms result in minor impairment in social, school or work settings.

Moderate: Symptoms or functional impairment between 'mild' and 'severe' are present.

Severe: Many symptoms are present beyond the number needed to make a diagnosis; several symptoms are particularly severe; or symptoms result in marked impairment in social, school or work settings.

As individuals age, their symptoms may lessen, change or take different forms. For example, during adolescence, signs of hyperactivity (e.g., running and climbing) are less common and may be confined to fidgeting or inner feelings of restlessness or impatience.

ADHD is more than just Attention Deficit!

MORE FACTS: ADHD is a neurobiological (brain) condition with genetic and environmental causes that impacts on performance (Barkley, Russell A., 2013). This condition often leaves parents and teachers baffled when children with ADHD, including those who are intellectually gifted, are barely making school grades.

The current understanding is that deficits in 'Executive Functioning' (EF) (mental skills needed when pursuing goals) that make it difficult to succeed in school and socially, is the main shortfall in ADHD.

Russell Barkley, Ph.D., who has been at the forefront of exploring the relationship between ADHD and EF, says that EF poses more of a problem with doing what one knows, rather than one of knowing what to do. It is a performance vs. knowledge (distinction). Given that executive functioning and ADHD are tightly linked, children with ADHD (even if they try hard) will fall short and struggle with the following:

- Controlling emotions
- Shifting from one task to another
- Poor working memory

- Remembering and following multi-step instructions

- Staying on track

- Planning and organising materials and assignments

- Balancing tasks, such as sports and academic demands

- Completing tasks in a timely fashion

- Applying previously learned information to solve problems

- Asking for help or more information, when needed

- Self-monitoring

As the brain continues to develop, the symptoms of executive functioning issues may change. Early intervention is best as it can help the individual find ways to use his/her strengths to support weaknesses. However, since the brain continues to develop into young adulthood, intervention can be helpful at any age.

The following components of EF are adapted from the work of Barkley, (2012) & Brown, (2005).

- **Impulse control:** This is a child's ability to stop and think before acting. Impulsivity can be a symptom of ADHD. Children who have trouble with impulse control may blurt things out. They may do unsafe things without thinking them through. They also may quit a chore halfway through to go hang out with friends, and have trouble following rules consistently.

- **Emotional control:** This is a child's ability to manage his/her feelings by focusing on the end result or goal. Children who struggle with emotional control often are more sensitive to criticism. They also may overreact to little injustices and struggle to separate emotions and actions.

- **Flexibility:** This is a child's ability to 'roll with the punches' and come up with new approaches when a plan fails. Children who are inflexible think in very concrete ways. They don't see other options or solutions. They find it difficult to change course.

- **Working memory:** This is a child's ability to hold information in his/her mind and use it to complete a task. Children who have weak working memory skills have trouble with multi-step tasks. They have a hard time remembering directions, taking notes or understanding something just explained to them.

- **Self-monitoring:** This is a child's ability to keep track of and evaluate his/her performance on regular tasks. Children who have trouble self-monitoring lack self-awareness. They can't tell if their strategies are working. They may not even realise they have strategies. They often don't know how to check their progress.

- **Organisation:** This is a child's ability to keep track of information and things. Children with organisational issues are constantly losing or misplacing things. They can't find a way to get organised, even when there are negative consequences to being disorganised.

- **Planning and prioritising:** This is a child's ability to come up with the steps needed to reach a goal and to decide their order of importance. Children with weak planning and prioritising skills may not know how to start a project. They may be easily overwhelmed trying to break tasks into smaller, more manageable chunks. They may have trouble seeing the main idea.

- **Task initiation:** This is a child's ability to get started on something. Children who struggle with this skill often have issues with planning and prioritising as well. Without having a plan for a task, it's hard to know how to start. Children with task initiation problems can come across as 'lazy' or as 'procrastinators'. But often they're just so overwhelmed that they freeze and do nothing.

If you are struggling with any of the above issues, it may feel distressing, but there are strategies that you can learn to help you manage your ADHD challenges. Talk to your parents, and be open about seeking and accepting help.

*"I don't mean to interrupt people.
I just randomly remember things and get really excited."*

Anonymous

Take Away: **ADHD has many faces that impact children differently. Unfortunately, ADHD rarely exists in isolation, with more children than not having at least one other disorder. It is estimated that approximately two thirds of children with ADHD have at least one other mental disorder, and as many as ten percent have three or more disorders. The coexisting disorder has a significant influence on how ADHD symptoms affect mood, behaviour and academic functioning. Treatment will vary depending on the secondary disorder.**

Kids with ADHD need someone in their corner. Even if you don't always have the answer, be that someone.

How is ADHD diagnosed?

Tristan arrived in good spirits and told me that he had achieved an 'A' for a maths test. He was especially chuffed because his grade was higher than the smartest boy in the class. Also, as a reward, Mrs Smart had given him a voucher for the school canteen.

Tris: Mum's made an appointment to see Dr Brainy. He seems very busy and can only see us in eight weeks. If someone cancels, mum said that they'll call her. Did you also have to wait so long to see Dr Cool?

Xavier: I can't remember exactly how long I waited, but I understand that people wait anything between four to twelve weeks to see a paediatrician like Dr Cool – that's a doctor who specialises in working with children up to the age of eighteen.

Tris: Is there anything that Mum and I can do while we wait?

Xavier: Yeah! You've already started – you're learning as much as you can about ADHD! Every month my mum goes to a support group for parents of children with ADHD. I'll get more information about it, in case your mum wants to attend. By the way, does your mum know that you are having these meetings with me?

Tris: No! I haven't told anyone. But I was wondering whether mum could come with me one day. Maybe she can leave work earlier on Friday! Would that be OK with you? But not quite yet!

Xavier: Yeah, no worries! You just tell me when. The plan is that we meet for a total of eight Fridays. You can decide when you would like your mum to join us.

Tris: I think that she is going to be super happy to know that I am seeing you. So, what else did Dr Cool tell you besides your ADHD type and prescribing medication?

Xavier: I remember him telling me that there are many children in Australia with ADHD. He said that there were probably other children at my school who had ADHD too.

Tris: Too right! I reckon I am one of them! I wonder if there are more?

Xavier: I now know of at least another five. One of them comes to have a chat with me when he needs; the others I don't really know, but my mother knows their mothers as they all go to the same support group.

Tris: By the way, what do they talk about in the parents' support group?

Xavier: Not quite sure! But I think that it's more about supporting each other with information and resources, so that they can, in turn, help us.

Tris: Ok! I've been wondering, is it only boys who have ADHD?

Xavier: Not at all. Boys, as well as girls, can have ADHD. Girls might not be diagnosed as early as boys, because they often are not as disruptive and don't attract the teachers' attention as having major problems. I read somewhere that three boys, to every one girl, are diagnosed with ADHD.

Tris: Phew! That's a lot of boys! Wow, it's 3:30 already... time goes by so fast in here – I will see you next week at the same time. Cheers!

Xavier: Cheers! Have a good weekend.

FACT: ADHD is a relatively common diagnosis, but that doesn't mean it should be taken lightly. ADHD may be compared to an iceberg: most of the problems are hidden beneath the surface and only the tip of the problem is visible (Zeigler, A. 2011). Typically, teachers and parents see the obvious tip first, the behaviour problems, such as failing to complete homework, back-chatting and arguing.

Yet, for so many children this condition is much more complex. School can be incredibly difficult because of inattention, impulsiveness, executive function deficits and other serious learning problems. Remember, that up to two-thirds of children with ADHD have at least one other diagnosable condition that often has a significant impact on schoolwork.

Given that there's no single, definitive diagnostic test for ADHD – no blood analysis, no brain scan, no genetic screening – diagnosis of ADHD should not be a quick, simple task.

Often, the ADHD diagnosis begins with an 'Aha' moment, when it dawns on parents that their child's challenges may be caused by ADHD or another biologically-based disorder. This 'Aha' moment might come when a teacher expresses concern that a child is being disruptive in class or falling behind academically. Whatever triggers an 'Aha' moment, it needs to be addressed and help needs to be sought. Without a prompt diagnosis, individuals with ADHD are likely to be branded, 'lazy', 'careless', or worse. Such labels undermine self-esteem and can lead to years of under-achievement and family turmoil.

In Australia this 'Aha' moment needs to be followed up by an appointment with your General Practitioner (GP), for a discussion and a written referral to a Paediatrician or Child Psychiatrist (ideally one who has an interest in ADHD). Not all GPs are trained in the complexities of ADHD and its overlapping conditions, but they can facilitate the management of the condition. Professionals trained in diagnosing ADHD routinely screen for these problems and are equipped to perform the in-depth evaluation needed.

Diagnosing ADHD

When making an accurate diagnosis, a specialist will first want to determine whether a child has the ADHD symptoms listed in *The Diagnostic and Statistical Manual of Mental Disorders-Fifth Edition (DSM-5)*. According to the *DSM-5* guidelines, to be diagnosed with ADHD, a child must have at least six of the nine symptoms of inattention and/or hyperactivity/impulsivity prior to age twelve. In addition, these symptoms must be causing problems in the child's functioning in more than one setting – home, school, or work.

While the *DSM-5* outlines the basics for an ADHD diagnosis, there's much more to arriving at an accurate diagnosis. In addition to reviewing these criteria, doctors need to conduct a thorough clinical interview. Thomas Brown, assistant clinical professor of psychiatry says, "The clinical interview is the core of any evaluation, the more input from different sources, the better." Individuals diagnosed with ADHD are often found to have a number of other disorders besides their ADHD (Barkley, 2006; Brown, 2011). As many as 87% of clinically diagnosed ADHD children may have at least one other disorder and 67% have at least two other disorders (Kadesjo & Gillberg, 2001). Results for adults with ADHD are nearly as high, with more than 80% having at least one disorder and more than 50% having two or more (Barkley et al., 2008). The disorders likely to co-occur with ADHD include:

Disruptive Behavioural Disorders: More than 50% of ADHD children meet criteria for a disruptive behavioural disorder (MTA Cooperative Group 1999). Even in the absence of a full diagnosis, the lives of many children with ADHD are afflicted by lying, defiance, blaming others and being easily angered. The three conditions that compromise disruptive behavioural disorders are; oppositional, conduct, and antisocial disorders.

Anxiety and Mood Disorders: Anxiety disorders occur in 34% of children with ADHD (MTA Cooperation Group 1999), but according to Bernstein and Layne (2004) half of these children never tell their parents. These individuals are overcome, most days, by painful worries without obvious triggers. Children may appear edgy, stressed out, tense and have sleep issues. They may also experience panic attacks.

In relation to mood disorders, according to Brown, T (2000), between 15% and 75% of those with ADHD may have a mood disorder. Worth noticing is that although children with ADHD get depressed briefly, they flow with the environment, whereas depressed children stay depressed for longer periods of time. The symptoms include loss of joy, sadness, pervasive irritability, withdrawal, and self-critical outlook. Sleep problems is a prominent symptom for both depression and anxiety.

Tic Disorders and Tourette's Disorder: ADHD frequently co-occurs in children with Tourette Syndrome. Less than 10% of those with ADHD have Tourette's, but 60% to 80% of children with Tourette Syndrome have ADHD. The ADHD diagnosis usually precedes the onset of the motor or vocal tics of Tourette's, although sometimes the two occur together. Some children with ADHD may develop a simple motor tic disorder (throat clearing, sniffling, eye blinking, neck stretching), that first appears during the course of their treatment for ADHD. While these two conditions appear linked in time, most experts believe that the co-occurrence in most cases is purely coincidental and not caused by ADHD or its treatment (*DSM-5*).

Assessing for ADHD in Children

- **Time:** An initial consultation could range from thirty minutes to one hour, or more. This time should be spent with the child as well as the parents, looking for signs of ADHD, and for other possible explanations for the symptoms. Your doctor may also arrange for intelligence tests or memory recall tests.

- **Questionnaires:** Expect to fill out questionnaires, checklists, and/or ADHD rating scales. Parents, teachers, and caregivers, will be asked to fill them out as well. The more input, the more likely an accurate diagnosis.

- **Medical Examination:** This should include screening for hearing and vision problems to rule out physical causes for symptoms.

- **Social History:** Have you moved a lot? Are there financial challenges in the family? Is there a family member who is ill? These and other factors can make the child anxious — and may cause behaviour that mimics ADHD.

- **Family History:** ADHD runs in families, so the doctor may ask parents questions about their own mental health. According to Dr Dodson, a psychiatrist specialising in adults with ADHD, "If one parent has ADHD, there's a 50-50 chance that the child has it too. If both parents have ADHD, it is a major contributor."

- **Symptom History:** A child has to exhibit at least six of nine symptoms of inattention and/or hyperactivity/ impulsivity prior to age twelve in order to be diagnosed with ADHD (*DSM-5*). In addition, the symptoms should be exhibited in more than one setting (school, home, work), to a point where the symptoms affect normal functioning.

Harold Meyer, founder of 'The A.D.D. Resource Centre', suggests the following tips in preparation for a comprehensive and responsible evaluation of ADHD:

- **Be specific when describing your problems:** Discuss with your parents what concerns you want to address in your consultation. For instance, "I can't follow instructions","I complete my homework but then lose it", "I get angry and blame others".

- **Discuss your view on medication with your parents before your appointment:** If you don't want to take medication, state your concerns up front and ask your doctor if he/she can recommend other treatment options. The decision to take medication is entirely up to you and your parents. If your doctor writes a prescription, despite your aversion to medication, don't be afraid to see someone else for a second opinion! If you have decided on medication, remember that the prescription and dosing process varies with each individual. It's likely that you'll need to try more than one type, and experiment with different dosages, to find the right one for you.

- **Ask your doctor about medication options:** You want someone who does not just write a prescription, but who will also discuss the diagnosis and treatment process in detail. The following questions should be addressed: Why start with a particular medication? What can you expect to happen? How should you evaluate the effect of the medication?

- **Discuss follow-up:** Your doctor should outline a course of action, including treatment and follow-up appointments. Ask about his/her accessibility as you work with your parents to find the right medication and dosage for you.

- **Learn about alternatives to medication:** Find out about behavioural therapies and modifications you can try. Can your doctor work with you on these? Is your doctor open to non-medical treatment? You may benefit from a referral to a psychologist who can offer behavioural strategies, such as ways to deal with problems at school, at work, time-management techniques, and so on.

- **Ask your doctor whether he/she will meet with your family, if the need arises:** A diagnosis of ADHD affects those you live with. They also need to learn about the condition and how it will be managed.

How quickly can an ADHD diagnosis be made?

If you're awaiting a diagnosis, inform your teachers or ask your parents to arrange a meeting with your teachers and any other school officials that are part of your evaluation process. According to Silver, L., (2005), learning disorders affects 30% to 50% of children with ADHD. Given this, if you suspect that you have more than just ADHD, ask your parents to request an assessment designed to identify learning, language, motor, or organisation/executive function problems. You may also need to pursue a clinical evaluation to determine if you are living with anxiety, depression, anger control, OCD, or a tic disorder.

At this point, you might be a little anxious to know whether you have ADHD or not. But don't expect an answer overnight. The diagnostic process typically takes at least a week or two. The most important aspect of the process is that it is thorough and carried out responsibly.

What a diagnosis can mean

If you are diagnosed with ADHD, you now know that your problem is a genuine medical condition. That, in itself, can lift a huge load off your shoulders. This information gives insight into school, social and family problems. Your parents, too, may feel a sense of relief. They now know that your learning, concentration, and attention problems are not the result of 'bad parenting'.

For your siblings and friends, a diagnosis of ADHD means that there is a real reason – not just a negative attitude, poor motivation, or carelessness – for your behaviours. It also means that things probably will be less tense and stressful at home and at school, once treatment begins.

For teachers, a diagnosis of ADHD means that they can make classroom changes and accommodations (implement different strategies, techniques and instructional practice) to help you become more successful in school. Generally, diagnosis is a win-win situation for everyone.

Some parents get diagnosed with ADHD during the process of having their children diagnosed. Available evidence suggests that ADHD is genetic — passed down from parent to child. A child with ADHD is four times more likely to have a relative with ADHD. One father commented, "While completing my son's screening questionnaire, I found myself leaping from the pages. The condition affecting my son had been affecting me my all life."

ADHD and Gender

According to clinical psychologist, Thomas Brown, boys with ADHD often behave in ways that are tough for teachers to ignore. This helps explain why boys are three times more likely to be diagnosed with ADHD than their female peers and also why boys tend to get diagnosed at younger ages than girls. On average, girls with ADHD are diagnosed five years later than boys — boys at age seven and girls at age twelve. There are also many girls who never get diagnosed. Research indicates as many as 75% of girls with attention issues are undiagnosed. This disparity isn't necessarily because girls are less susceptible to the disorder. Rather, it's likely because ADHD symptoms present differently in girls. Boys are more likely to have significant hyperactivity and impulsivity, while girls can present with inattention and distractibility.

Girls with ADHD are often labeled 'daydreamers' — think of the girl who sits quietly in class, looking out the window while playing with her hair. Boys with ADHD are typically disruptive in the classroom and cause trouble on the playground. They usually show externalised symptoms, such as impulsivity. Girls, on the other hand, typically show internalised symptoms. These symptoms include inattentiveness and low self-esteem.

Boys also tend to be more physically aggressive, while girls tend to be more verbally aggressive. That's why so often it's the boys who are referred by teachers for testing. The old saying of 'the squeaky wheel gets the grease' still prevails.

Research in this field suggests that undiagnosed ADHD can have a negative impact on girls' self-esteem and puts girls at an increased risk for depression, anxiety and eating disorders. Girls with undiagnosed ADHD are also more likely to have problems in school, social settings, and personal relationships. Typical symptoms in girls include:

- being withdrawn
- difficulty with academic achievement
- inattentiveness or a tendency to daydream
- low self-esteem
- anxiety
- intellectual impairment

- trouble focusing

- appearing not to listen

- verbal aggression, such as teasing, taunting, or name-calling

- eating disorders

Although more often misdiagnosed in girls, ADHD can be missed in boys as well. Traditionally, boys are seen as more energetic, so if they run around and act out, it may be dismissed as simply 'boys being boys'.

Studies show that boys with ADHD report more hyperactivity and impulsivity than girls. But it's a mistake to assume that all boys with ADHD are hyperactive or impulsive. Some boys display the inattentive aspects of the disorder. They may not be diagnosed, because they aren't physically disruptive. Boys with ADHD tend to display the symptoms that most people think of when they imagine ADHD behaviour. These include:

- impulsivity or 'acting out'

- talking excessively

- hyperactivity, such as running and hitting

- lack of focus, including inattentiveness

- inability to sit still

- physical aggression

- frequently interrupting other peoples' conversations and activities

If you suspect that you have ADHD, speak to your parents or make an appointment with your GP for an evaluation as soon as possible. Getting a prompt diagnosis and treatment can greatly improve symptoms. It can also help prevent other problems from developing in the future.

"I was never impulsive or hyperactive.
So, it never occurred to me that I might have ADHD."

– Client

Take Away: **If you are questioning whether you have ADHD or not, speaking to your GP is a good first step. GPs cannot officially diagnose ADHD, but they are the link between you and your Paediatrician or Psychiatrist, who are the only professionals in Australia who can make an official diagnosis of ADHD, and prescribe medication.**

"Remember that you are not alone. There are others going through the same thing."

Adam Levine,
lead singer of Maroon 5

CHAPTER FOUR

Life On The Home Front

Tristan arrived at 3:15 and was not in a good mood. Mrs Smart had kept him behind because he had spoken out of turn a couple of times. He felt that other children also spoke out of turn sometimes, and that they didn't get punished. I used this incident to explore some of Tristan's values around fairness. I also helped Tris understand the link between actions, thoughts and feelings. This helped him understand that it wasn't so much Mrs Smart's action that was causing his anger, but rather *his thought* that she had treated him differently to the way she treated the other children in the class when they talked out of turn.

Xavier: Glad that you still decided to come, mate! Do you want to talk about anything specific today?

Tris: I think you can just tell me more about what to expect from my doctor. When you look back, was it a good thing to get a diagnosis and take medication? Was it the best thing that could have happened to you?

Xavier: In relation to my ADHD, without a doubt it was a good thing. For the first time, at the age of thirteen, I realised that I was not stupid or lazy. Dr Cool said that the problems I was having were not my fault. He said that when children have ADHD, their brains work a little different from children who don't have ADHD. He also said that it's like having a car with the accelerator stuck on.

Tris: That's a bit like me! My body moves before I know what it's doing and words come out of my mouth before I think about them, like today with Mrs Smart. I feel frustrated and mad a lot of the time. Dad didn't understand, so I got belted often.

Xavier: Well, I had the toughest time with my dad too! He is a super clever accountant, but didn't understand ADHD. To him, I was just lazy and didn't try hard enough.

Tris: At least you have a dad! Mine was a FIFO worker. You know what FIFO is, right? It stands for 'Fly In Fly Out' work, where people work away from home for a set period of time, then they go home and then they go back to work, and on it goes. Well, one day he left for work and never came back. He just left – that was four years ago. Mum and Dad argued all the time, and mostly about me... Mum has been through a lot with me.

Xavier: Sorry that your dad left; happens a lot I guess! My mum has always supported me, even with all my anger issues often directed at her. She was the one who took me to Dr Cool and every week to Joy. She also went on a parenting course, and saw a psychologist who understood about parenting children with ADHD.

Tris: It's OK! At least I have my Pop. He's kind, and I respect him and my Nanna. They always help mum and me – I sometimes worry because they are getting old.

Xavier: You're so lucky – my grandparents live overseas, so I never get to see them.

Tris: By the way, I gave the support group information to mum yesterday and I also told her that I was having these meetings with you on Fridays. She was so proud of me for doing this, and would really like to meet you to have a chat and say thank you. Can I invite her to come in with me next Friday?

29

Xavier: Next Friday is good for me! I'll come to school by bike, so I don't have to catch the bus in case we need more time. Have a good weekend!

Tris: You too!

FACT: Generally, being a parent is rewarding, but it's also hard work. Parents of children with ADHD question their parenting ability and may, at times, feel that they are unable to manage the complexity of their teen's difficulties. Siblings may feel neglected and resentful of the child with ADHD. Parents often:

- blame themselves
- experience denial, grief, anger, or disappointment
- become more irritable
- feel like failures because they can't control their children's behaviour
- have more conflict with their child with ADHD, especially if their child is also defiant.
- feel socially isolated because of their child's behaviour
- experience more conflict in their marriage or relationship with their partner, especially if they are not on the same page in terms of parenting values.

Given the above, support for parents is very important for long-term coping. Parent training, individual and family counselling is, at times, needed and often recommended, especially when depression or anxiety is present, and also to help the parent remain the parent that they would like their child to become (to be a good role model). To do this, the parents need to accept the following three facts:

- ADHD cannot be 'cured' because there is nothing to cure; it's not an illness or a disease.
- Teens are going to be challenging in many ways – it is simply 'part and parcel' of this developmental phase.
- Probably, it is not so much the **strategies** that need changing, but rather the **mindset**.

During the teen years, the 'job description' for parents and for teens seems to be in conflict. Parents' primary job is to gradually decrease their control, letting go of their teenager with care and skill. On the other hand, the teenager's main job, for better or worse, is to experiment with making his/her own decisions, testing limits, and managing freedom.

In some cases, when the teen starts this process, parents may feel that they are 'losing control' and ironically, the natural tendency is to exert even more control – often with dire consequences. When a teen has ADHD, things are even more complicated for a number of reasons:

Emotional immaturity: Children with ADHD are more immature emotionally than their peers without ADHD. Some experts indicate that this discrepancy can be as much as 30%, meaning that an eighteen-year-old may have the emotional maturity of a thirteen-year-old. Many parents of children with ADHD will agree that maturity levels fluctuate; one day their teen may act like an eighteen-year-old and the next day seem as if he/she is thirteen. They are more impulsive than their peers without ADHD, and seldom think of consequences before they act. Chronologically, teenagers are ready to assume their independence. Unfortunately, developmentally, they are not.

Discipline methods: Parents of children with ADHD soon realise that traditional discipline methods rarely work. They don't learn from rewards and punishment and have a difficult time connecting discipline with behaviours, unless the punishment is immediate. Methods that may have worked when children were younger, such as behavioural charts and time-outs, are not effective during the teen years. The emotional immaturity and a low frustration tolerance can lead to frequent blow-ups and angry outbursts. This can leave the parents feeling that 'nothing works anymore' and without currency. When this happens, it is very important for the parent to realise that although their teen's life may be spinning out of control, they don't have to go down, as well. This may be the time to 'put the oxygen mask on yourself first' and then seek support.

Mood disorders: Because children and teens with ADHD frequently have mood disorders, such as anxiety, depression or bipolar disorder, finding the right treatment plan can be difficult. These problems only add to a teen's frustration at not being able to become independent, and a parent's frustration at not feeling their teen is ready for steps toward independence.

Learning disabilities: While ADHD is not a learning disability, it can cause difficulty in learning. Some teens have additional learning disabilities, causing problems in school. These problems increase a teen's feeling of 'being different' or not being accepted by their peers. Parents may feel they still need to be hyper-vigilant in keeping up with schoolwork, homework, tests and projects. They may still communicate with teachers on a weekly basis. All this makes your teen feel like a child. While your teen craves independence, being so dependent on a parent's help can create frustration and resentment.

Self-esteem: Living with ADHD can be challenging. Many teens with ADHD find that the school environment does not suit their personality or maximise their natural talents. It is important for the teens to find an environment and activities that reminds them of their strengths, and allows them to experience success. Important, too, is to remember that everyone has strengths and weaknesses, regardless of whether they have ADHD or not.

While the teen years are frustrating, they don't need to be impossible. Remembering the positive sides of ADHD, teaching your teen advocacy skills and working with the doctor to refine your teen's treatment plan, can make these years a little more manageable.

There will be obstacles. There will be doubters. There will be mistakes. But with hard work... There are no limits.

Michael Phelps

Take Away:

- **Keep lines of communication open. Discussing issues in the heat of the moment when everyone is angry doesn't work. Instead, set aside a time when all parties are calm to discuss any areas of disagreement or conflict.**

- **Meet your teen where he/she is developmentally, rather than setting expectations based on chronological age.**

- **Keep your expectations and your child's reality in check.**

- **Support your teen to understand and manage his/her ADHD, so he/she can have the confidence to advocate for himself/herself and thrive to be the incredible adult that he/she can be, despite having ADHD.**

- **If family conflict is taking a large toll on the family, consider seeking help from a qualified mental health professional.**

> *A child needs encouragement like a plant needs water.*
>
> Rudolph Dreikurs

Getting Help For ADHD

Tristan arrived in a cheerful mood; he was particularly happy that his mum was on her way to join us, and told me that she had gone to the support group for the first time on the Wednesday.

Tris: This is my mum, Catherine.

Xavier: Nice to meet you, and thank you for coming in today.

Catherine: Nice to meet you, Xavier, and thank you so much for all the time you're giving to Tristan. Fridays have become his best day of the week! Is that right, Tristan?

Tris: I guess so!

Xavier: Tristan tells me that you attended the support group. How was it?

Catherine: It was really good! I enjoyed being around other parents who are experiencing similar challenges, and it was very informative as well. I will most certainly try to attend as many groups as work allows.

Xavier: That's great, and I'm happy that you found it informative. So, Tris, is there anything on your mind that you would like to talk about, or is it mum's time today?

Tris: Is there anything you want to ask Xavier, mum? Can I play games when I get home, pleeease?

Catherine: We will discuss it later, Tristan! Well, where do I start?

Xavier: How about I take two minutes to tell you a little about myself first? I'll set the timer, otherwise it becomes ten minutes. Firstly, as Tris most probably has told you, I have ADHD. I was diagnosed four years ago, at the same age as Tris. When I was fifteen, I did a Peer Mentoring course, and now I help kids in our school who are experiencing challenges in their lives, not just with ADHD.

Catherine: Thank you so much for that! What you do makes such a difference. I can see the positive impact that it is having on Tristan. Has Tristan told you that he has an appointment to see the Paediatrician in six weeks?

Xavier: Yes, he did! We've been talking about my first appointment with Dr Cool, my Paediatrician, in preparation for Tristan's first appointment. As I told Tris, getting diagnosed was the best thing that happened to me. My life has changed so much since then. I attribute the positive change in my life to four things; getting diagnosed, medication, counselling and the satisfaction I experience volunteering as a peer mentor.

Don't get me wrong! I still have many challenges, but I choose to change what is under my control, like my attitude and how I spend my time. And to accept what is not under my control, like my diagnosis of ADHD, other peoples' attitudes and behaviour, school rules etc.

Catherine: That is such a good attitude to have and so good to hear! Most things I've heard about ADHD were negative. When Mrs Smart mentioned that

Tristan may have ADHD, my heart sank. I blamed myself and wondered where I had gone wrong as a parent. Oh my! Look at the time – already 3:45. I can see why Tristan tells me that time goes very quickly in here. You've been very quiet, Tristan.

Tris: It's Ok! I have a list of stuff to ask Xavier next Friday, so no worries. We better go, Mum. Xavier needs to go too. Can I play the game, Mum?

Xavier: It's Ok! I have until four o'clock today.

Tris: In that case, can you please tell my mum about the different types of ADHD, and the combination of treatments that work for you?

Xavier: Sure can! Here is a fact sheet on the three types of ADHD – it's self-explanatory. As for treatment, Dr Cool told Mum and me that when managing ADHD, no treatment on its own is sufficient, and that using a combination of treatments to get the best outcome possible is needed. They call it a multimodal approach. So, Mum and I decided on a combination of medication and counselling for me, and she did a parenting course. The medication that Dr Cool prescribed helped me concentrate and focus better. I also felt less fidgety, and my head felt clearer.

Tris: What about counselling?

Xavier: I enjoyed counselling! Joy was all about life skills! She first taught me about ADHD then she helped me to challenge what she calls 'poisonous thoughts' (negative thoughts). She also helped me to realise that life is all about choices and that avoiding things does not make them go away. I especially enjoyed exploring my values, identifying what really matters to me in life, and how this can be helpful when setting goals. We played a cool game called the 'Game of Life'. She also taught me skills to better manage my time, not get so distracted, procrastinate less and how to problem-solve.

Tris: What if my doctor doesn't send me to someone like Joy?

Catherine: I am sure that we can ask him or find one ourselves. Maybe Dr Maddie can send us to someone she knows.

Xavier: I can also give you Joy's card, and you can contact her directly if you want. Her office is in the city.

Tris: That's cool, then! How many times did you see Dr Cool and Joy?

Xavier: I see Dr Cool at least twice a year for a follow-up, just to make sure that the medication is still working. He has changed my medication a couple of times.

I saw Joy every week for about three months, when I was first diagnosed, then once a month for about a year. Now, I make an appointment to see her when I need to. It's good to know there's someone out there who understands me, and my 'stuff'.

Tris: Do you still need medication now that you have learned how to not be aggressive, and stuff?

Xavier: That is a very clever question! In my case I do still need medication because I find that a combination of medication and using the techniques that Joy taught me work best to help me stay on track. I get better grades, life at home has improved, and I am happier and more confident.

> Time's up! Again, thank you so much for everything Xavier – you are a great mentor! Tristan is lucky to have met you.

> You are most welcome! See you next Friday, Tris!

FACT: Although no cure currently exists for ADHD, this doesn't mean that nothing can be done about it. Successful treatment generally involves a combination of education, therapy and medication (multidisciplinary). Although the symptoms of ADHD may change with age, many individuals still need treatment into adulthood.

Education is a necessary component to any effective treatment plan and provides the information to understand and manage the disorder. With a childhood diagnosis the education is often directed at the parents. However, it is very important that as the child gets older and more independent from the parents, that he/she increases their own knowledge about ADHD and takes responsibility for the management thereof.

Multidisciplinary approach: The treatment of ADHD requires a comprehensive behavioural, psychological, educational, and medical evaluation, followed by education of the individual and their family members as to the nature of the disorder and the methods proven to assist with its management (Barkley & Murphy 2006). Combined pharmacological and cognitive/behavioural interventions remain the best treatment options for most children with ADHD (Phelam et el., 2014). Key elements of a multidisciplinary approach include:

- Medication

- Psychological Interventions (e.g individual, parental and group therapy)

- Coaching

- Support for any coexisting conditions, especially Learning Disorders which can be overlooked as a symptom of ADHD, rather than a problem that needs to be addressed independently of the ADHD.

Medication: Medication is often the first line of treatment in ADHD, because it can be highly effective in the treatment of the core symptoms of ADHD – Inattention, Hyperactivity and Impulsivity (medication seems to work for 75% to 90% of children who try the medication). However, medication does not provide individuals with concrete strategies and skills to cope with peer relationships, social struggles and other disruptions in quality of life – such as underachieving and parental conflict (Safren, et al., 2005). Benefits seem to be short-lived and only present while the medication is active in the body. Once the medication wears off, the benefits disappear. Despite medication treatment, most adolescents continue to experience residual symptoms, thus necessitating the need for evidence-based psychological treatments, in addition to medication, in order to provide a comprehensive treatment (Phelam et el., 2014).

Controversy continues to exist around the medications used to treat ADHD. These medications are seen, by some, as powerful drugs that can have major side effects and possibly lead to addiction. Despite these negative views, studies show that medications used to treat ADHD are not, in themselves, addictive. When they are prescribed by a responsible and knowledgeable professional and taken responsibly as prescribed, there is little chance that too much medication may be given or taken. Responsible doctors will monitor the dosage and side effects of the medication with frequent follow-ups.

Therapy/Counselling: According to Dr David Rabiner, a child clinical psychologist, non-medical interventions for teens with ADHD is important for several reasons, as follows:

- As many as 20%–30% of adolescents with ADHD do not benefit significantly from medication and/or continue to struggle, despite the help that medication provides.

- Others experience adverse side effects that deter them from staying on medication.

- In addition to these limitations of medication treatment, many teens refuse to stay on ADHD medication, and adherence to medication treatment typically declines with age.

- Finally, diversion of medication is a problem, as it is not uncommon for teens taking ADHD meds to be approached by peers looking to use their medication for their own benefit (i.e. to improve their performance at exam time).

A typical Cognitive Behavioural Therapy (CBT) program for tweens/teens covers the following: *Adapted from; (Sprich, E. Susan; Burbridge, S.; Lemer, A. Jonathan; Safren, A. Steven, 2015).*

Psychoeducation: Provides psychoeducation about ADHD and introduces the CBT model of treatment of ADHD.

Organisation and Planning: Teaches tweens/teens the benefits of developing and maintaining a diary/notebook with a task list and a calendar system to improve their organisation for school assignments. It includes a strong focus on problem-solving skills, such as breaking large tasks into smaller and more manageable steps. Teens also learn to develop an action plan for overwhelming tasks.

Reducing Distractibility: The focus here is on helping teens reduce their tendency to become distracted. Teens are taught to recognise the length of time they can hold their attention to tasks and to divide tasks into chunks that do not exceed this time. Teens are also taught to use tools, such as alarms and timers, to help stay on task. They also learn a technique called 'distractibility delay' that involves writing down distractions, when they emerge, as opposed to acting on them in the moment.

Adaptive thinking: Here teens are taught skills to maximise adaptive thinking during times of stress, and to apply adaptive thinking skills to difficulties associated with ADHD. For example, take a teen who becomes highly self-critical when he/she forgets to turn in an assignment and who thinks that he/she will never master the organisation problems associated with ADHD and thus will never be successful. One can imagine how such thinking can contribute to 'giving up', low self-esteem, and even to the emergence of depressive symptoms. In this example the teen is taught to challenge these self-critical thoughts and to consider alternatives. For example, the therapist can point out that this was just one assignment he/she forgot to hand in and that he/she had been turning in most of his/her work. The goal is to help teens develop the skills to recognise when their thinking is overly negative, and to challenge that thinking with more adaptive alternatives. And to help him/her challenge the negative self-statements that get in the way of completing tasks or carrying out goals.

Anger and Frustration Management: Because anger is the emotion that gets teens into trouble the most, cognitive restructuring skills are used to help teens deal more appropriately with anger and frustration. Teens are taught stress reduction techniques, like mindfulness, and instructed on how to act assertively.

Reducing Procrastination: The focus here is on helping the teen apply previously-learned skills, like mindfulness and problem-solving, to manage and reduce procrastination tendency.

Improving Communication Skills: Teens are helped to identify their preferred style of communication and learn assertive communication skills. This includes the use of "I" statements – this skill reduces the likelihood of the child coming across as blaming during sensitive interactions and forces the child to take responsibility for his/her own feelings and thoughts. Another helpful technique is 'reflection' – a powerful communication tool that helps the child become a better listener by repeating back what someone has just said to them in their own words.

Where necessary, CBT can address other important issues that affect ADHD symptoms, such as co-existing mood and anxiety disorders, dependence on technology and gaming, career search, or overall lifestyle habits, such as sleep, exercise, and one's self-esteem. Solanto (2011), suggests that CBT is most effective when combined with other forms of treatment, such as medication, and further states that a therapist's role is to help individuals develop good habits and maintain them. She stresses the importance of providing support to encourage their use. The best measure of whether CBT is working comes from assessing outcomes in the individual's daily life.

Worth mentioning here is that of all the emotions that can get a child with ADHD into trouble, anger leads the list. While sadness or anxiety causes misery, it is anger that leads to trouble — punishment, suspension, expulsion, and a host of other outcomes we don't wish children to suffer. It is important that a child expresses his/her anger, but the emotion should be like 'a sneeze': It clears the passageways, and is over. A child who cannot get angry is in as much danger as a child who cannot control his/her anger.

"Do not teach your children never to be angry; teach them how to be angry."

– Lyman Abbott

The link between ADHD and Oppositional Defiant Disorder (ODD):

It is a fact that 40-50% of children with ADHD also have ODD, a condition marked by chronic aggression, frequent outbursts, and a tendency to argue, ignore requests, and engage in intentionally-annoying behaviour.

Although the reason so many children with ADHD exhibit oppositional behaviour is still not known, many experts suggest that ODD may be tied to ADHD-related impulsivity. According to Carol Bradly, a clinical psychologist, these children misbehave not because they're intentionally oppositional, but because they can't control their impulses. Some experts suggest that ODD is a way for kids to cope with the frustration and emotional pain associated with having ADHD. If left untreated, oppositional behaviour can evolve into conduct disorder, and more serious behavioural problems. It is therefore most important that help is sought.

The first step in managing ODD is making sure that the child's ADHD is under control. When a child's hyperactivity, impulsiveness and inattention are reduced, there is usually an improvement in ODD symptoms. It's also recommended that the therapist screens the child for anxiety, depression, and bipolar disorder, all of which can cause ODD and co-exist with ADHD.

Therapy to address ODD is often targeted at parents. The goal according to Barkley (2013) is to show the parents how to do the following:

- Recognise their own 'risk' factors, change them where possible, or at least try to prevent these factors from interfering with their effective management of their child.

- Recognise certain 'risk' factors in their child, attempt to change them where possible, or at least learn to accept those that cannot be changed, and strive to cope with them.

- Change the situational consequences they are providing for the child's non-compliance that often serve to create, maintain, or exacerbate defiant child behaviour.

Develop Lagging Executive Skills: Teens with ADHD may have been struggling not only with core ADHD symptoms of Inattention, Impulsivity and Hyperactivity, but also with chronic secondary symptoms, such as, managing time, procrastination, distractibility, disorganisation and difficulty following through on tasks. For many, these challenges lead to giving up, avoidance, anxiety and feelings of incompetence and underachievement. When working with teens with secondary symptoms, interventions that teach skills directly to the individual are most effective – this is a time when the teen is transitioning from close supervision to increased independence, adult supervision decreases, and environments that they transition into are often less structured. These interventions seek to help the adolescent rely less on their parents and more on their own cognitive and behavioural abilities to manage life in general.

Although some parental involvement is recommended in teaching these skills, at times this may not be possible, especially when communication between teen and parent has broken down and conflict is high. When this is the case, the teen may refuse parent involvement. For the sake of the therapeutic relationship and engagement, this wish needs to be respected – much to the frustration of some parents.

Working with an ADHD Coach: An ADHD coach knows about the specific, unique challenges facing teens with the condition and can help them acquire the skills to overcome those problems. Part cheerleader, part personal assistant, part teacher – a coach may help teens do the following:

- Develop structures for organising

- Make plans and set goals

- Get and stay motivated

- Develop time and money-management skills

- Offer suggestions, advice, reminders, and most importantly, encouragement

Some coaches meet with their clients weekly; others stay in regular contact by phone. Others meet with clients in their homes to help with specific tasks, such as organising papers or working on social skills.

Assessing for possible learning disabilities: According to Brown (2005), as much as 70% of children with ADHD have a learning disability. Given this, if a child continues to have academic difficulties (despite being treated for ADHD), an educational evaluation that assesses learning disabilities should be pursued.

Larry Silver (1999), says that learning disabilities can either exacerbate or mimic ADHD symptoms. If a learning disability exists and is not recognised early enough, the child may exhibit ADHD-like symptoms such as fidgeting, doodling, distractibility, that can mistakenly lead teachers and parents to conclude that the child has ADHD. Once the child is found to have a learning disorder, it's important to work closely with the school and ensure that recommendations on assessments are implemented.

> *"... There is nothing good or bad, but thinking makes it so."*
>
> *– William Shakespeare (Hamlet)*

Take Away: The primary message of a multimodal approach is that no single intervention, by itself, is sufficient to manage ADHD. The exact combination of treatment components will depend on how the child presents – ADHD has many faces. Therefore, there is no 'one size fits all'.

Alternative or Complementary Treatments

Some families choose to manage their child's symptoms in whole or in combination with medication and behaviour therapies, such as through diet, physical activity, and alternative therapies like meditation or brain training. However, the current scientific evidence on alternative therapies suggests that parents should be mindful and well-informed before they try these treatments. Some may cause side effects. Talk to your doctor before trying any alternative therapy for your child's ADHD.

Here's what we do know about the many treatments that have been promoted as alternatives to medication. Adapted from; (Chan et el., 2003):

- **Exercise:** Think of exercise as medication; exercise turns on the attention system, the so-called executive functions — sequencing, working memory, prioritising, inhibiting, and sustaining attention. On a practical level, it causes children to be less impulsive, which makes them more primed to learn. It's been shown that 30 minutes of exercise before school can help children with ADHD focus and manage moods.

- **Diet:** Changes in diet may help a small group of children who have allergy symptoms or migraine headaches. However, there is no evidence that a diet without sugar or additives will help the symptoms of ADHD. The most important thing is to eat a balanced diet; meaning one that comprises mainly fruits; vegetables; whole grains; proteins such as lean meats, poultry, fish, beans, eggs, and nuts; along with fat-free or low-fat dairy products low in saturated fats, trans fats, salt, and added sugars within your daily calorie needs.

- **Vitamin supplements:** If a child lacks a certain vitamin or mineral (such as iron, magnesium or zinc), a supplement may help. However, talk to your doctor about what amount is right for your child.

- **Fatty acids:** Essential fatty acids, such as fish oil and primrose oil, as well as 'nootropics', have not been shown to help children with ADHD.

- **Herbs:** Herbs can help calm a person, and they may play a role in memory and thinking. However, because herb products are not regulated, be sure to ask your pharmacist about the purity (its strength), safety, and toxicity (can it cause harm?) of any product.

- **Antioxidants:** Also known as anti-aging remedies, antioxidants protect nerve cells. But there is no direct effect on ADHD. Melatonin can help with sleep problems, but it can cause headaches, fatigue, irritability and sleepiness.

- **Homeopathy:** Homeopathy uses combinations of plant, animal or mineral extracts. No studies have shown that homeopathy is effective in treating ADHD. More research is needed.

- **Biofeedback:** Biofeedback is supposed to help people control their own responses. Studies on its effectiveness were undertaken with very small groups of children and the outcomes were not clear. It is still considered to be an experimental treatment.

- **Hypnotherapy:** Hypnotherapy might be helpful for certain symptoms of ADHD, such as sleep problems or tics.

- **Mindful Meditation and Yoga:** Mindful awareness, or mindfulness, involves paying close attention to your thoughts, feelings, and bodily sensations; in other words, developing a greater awareness from moment to moment. Studies found that children who participated in mindfulness exercises had lower test anxiety and fewer ADHD symptoms, plus greater attention than kids who did not participate in the exercises.

- **Vision therapy, oculovestibular treatment, sound training:** There is no evidence to support any of these treatments.

How to Approach ADHD Treatments

Most families of children with ADHD try a variety of treatment programs to maximise symptom control. If you plan to do this, keep a log, so you can follow the progress of your efforts and understand the outcomes of each strategy you try. Don't drop a treatment from your plan if changes aren't happening as fast as you'd like. Change takes time. Before you stop, unless side effects are getting in the way of your child's life, consult a professional. Look for ways to adjust the treatment before you give up on it.

How do I know when Medication is Working?

Most ADHD treatment plans need adjusting and may need reviewing several times before the ideal dosage is found. But one thing you should notice is an improvement in the level of your child's compliance, improved school grades as well as behavioural changes. Some children can't always tell when they act differently, and rely on their teachers and parents to monitor change. This monitoring is very important as it becomes the information that the treating specialist relies on in order to make responsible adjustments to the treatment plan.

Changes that clients report experiencing when medication is effective: Adapted from Chris, A. Zeigler, Dendy and Alex Zeigler (2007).

- Pay attention better
- Concentrate better
- Work quality is less erratic at school
- Get along better with friends and adults
- Do more schoolwork
- Make better grades
- Parents and teachers also report
    - o Less hyperactivity
    - o Less impulsivity
    - o Less arguing and backchat
    - o Less anger and aggression
    - o Less defiance

In order to put together the best treatment plan, your doctor may need to combine medications. This is especially so with co-existing conditions, such as anxiety and depression.

One of my clients said, "Before taking the medication I never really thought much about the past or the future. I pretty much just hopped from one activity to another without much reflection. Now, I can plan better and feel more in control of my life. It's as if the constant 'fog' lifted, and I can see things more clearly now."

"Understanding how you think is an effective start to making changes in your life."

– Russel Ramsay

Take Away: **When a child starts a new treatment plan, parents and health care providers should set goals related to academic, behavioural and social functioning. In other words, what needs improvement. Monitoring whether a treatment plan is moving the child closer to these goals is critical for a child's long-term success. Always being mindful that a child's response to treatment can, and does, change over time.**

CHAPTER SIX

When ADHD Goes Untreated

Tristan arrived early for our meeting. He now looked forward to these meetings and he had a whole bunch of questions for me. He also had a small gift for me from his mum. She could see a change in Tristan and she wanted to show her gratitude.

Xavier: Hi Tris. You're early today! Come on in.

Tris: My mum asked me to give you this!

Xavier: Thank you very much! I hope that your mum enjoyed our talk last week.

Tris: I think she really did! I overheard her tell Nanna and Pop about you – I also heard Pop say something about the side effects of ADHD medication. The whole week I was wondering if you had experienced side effects, and what you think would have happened if you'd refused to take medication.

Xavier: Yes, in fact I did! My appetite was affected, and I also struggled with sleep. Dr Cool assured us that it was normal and that it was common for children to experience some minor side effects. In my case, after I got used to the medication, my side effects disappeared. Part of the reason for the medical examination before diagnosis, is to screen for any existing medical conditions that may be aggravated by ADHD stimulant medication.

Tris: I think that Dr Maddie did all that when she gave Mum the referral for the Paediatrician.

Xavier: That's good then! And if you are diagnosed and decide to go on medication, any side effects will be managed by your doctor. Sometimes, modifying the dose and the time you take the medication is enough to stop the side effects. Dr Cool asked mum to keep a log book of the time that I took the medication, the time the side effects appeared, and a rating of my behaviour.

Tris: Did you have to take the medication at school?

Xavier: Yes, I did in the beginning and I did not like that at all. I had to go to the office at midday to take the second dose. I felt weird every time. Now, I think how silly it was of me to feel weird, but back then it was real. However, during our second visit to Dr Cool, after six months, Mum spoke to him about it and he changed the prescription to the 'slow release' version of the same medication, which meant that I only had to take one tablet in the morning before I went to school.

Tris: That's good to know. I don't think that I'd like to have to take medication at school either! Have you ever wondered what would've happened if you had refused to take the medication or your parents did not want you to be medicated?

Xavier: Obviously it's very difficult to know for sure! I can only guess. But, considering how things were — I would most probably have dropped out of school. The fighting with my parents over technology, homework, household chores, friends... everything really, would've gotten worse. Who knows where I would be today?

Tris: Do you still get angry and stuff?

Xavier: One very important thing that I learned is that anger is part of the many emotions that we all experience as humans. With Joy's help I realised that it was not getting angry that was getting me into trouble, but rather how I was managing my anger. To answer your question: Yes, I do still get angry, but I now have strategies that help me, especially breathing techniques.

Tris: Did you say breathing techniques?

Xavier: Well, it's actually called 'mindfulness'. People may call it many things, but essentially what it means is 'quietening the mind'. Earlier on you said that your mind, at times, felt like a washing machine on the 'spin cycle' – imagine trying to concentrate or do school work with your mind racing like that!

Tris: Well, I can't get anything done when I feel like that! All I do is feel angry and sad.

Xavier: Mindfulness information will be included in the Toolbox that I am putting together for you. We will go through all the tips, information and strategies in the last session, and you can ask any questions – as many as you like!

Tris: A Toolbox! Cool. Thank you. See you next Friday.

FACT: Many individuals think of ADHD as a condition that makes it difficult for children to pay attention or stay in their seats at school. But symptoms of ADHD affect children outside the classroom much more than is widely understood. And the consequences of untreated ADHD, even after children have finished school, can have a profound impact on their lives.

Some individuals with ADHD may have been previously diagnosed with depression, anxiety or learning disabilities. Although it is possible for these conditions to co-exist with ADHD, for some this previous diagnosis may stand in the way of discovering their ADHD. A complete medical history is important in order to differentiate diagnoses.

For example, when you have a headache, you know there are many possible causes, ranging from the mild to the more serious. When you see your doctor, she/he will likely ask you detailed questions about your headaches. Without a thorough assessment and examination, it would be irresponsible of your doctor to diagnose you with, say a brain tumor or stress (both can cause headaches). And, naturally, the treatment for a brain tumor and stress would look very different.

The same is true of mental illness. Many common symptoms occur for a variety of reasons, and can reflect several different diagnoses. That's why a good mental health professional will give your child a thorough evaluation based on a broad range of information before making a diagnosis. It's crucial to understand what's really behind a given behaviour, because just as in medicine, the diagnosis your child receives can drastically change the course of treatment. ADHD medications, for example, won't work if a child's inattention or disruptive behaviour is caused by anxiety and not ADHD. And when a treatment doesn't work, one of the things a good clinician needs to do is re-examine the diagnosis, as would a medical doctor.

Inattention, for example, is often first observed by teachers, who may notice a student who is unusually easily distracted, is prone to daydream, and has difficulty completing homework assignments and following directions. While many children (especially those who are very young) tend to have shorter attention spans than adults, some children have much more trouble focusing than others.

Inattention that is outside the typical range is one of the three core symptoms of ADHD, along with impulsivity, and hyperactivity. So, when a child seems unusually distracted, ADHD tends to be the first thing teachers, parents and clinicians suspect. However, there are many other possibilities that can be contributing to inattention. A child who is inattentive could be inattentive because he/she has ADHD, because he/she is worried about his/her mum who is undergoing cancer treatment, or because he/she is being bullied on the playground and does not know what to do about it.

From the above it is clear that a diagnosis of ADHD is not straight forward and needs to be taken seriously. Of importance, is for the individual to be honest and open with their doctor, explain why they believe they have ADHD, what symptoms are causing them the most problems and share as much as they can about their younger years of schooling or other experiences. This information is what the doctor will use to determine the best course of action.

Teenagers and young adults with untreated ADHD are often plagued with impulsivity, failure to think through the consequences of their decisions, an inability to finish what they start, and poor judgement. Statistics show that these individuals are more likely to abuse alcohol and drugs, more likely to get addicted, and to have early (and unprotected) sex, as well as being more likely to be expelled from school. They also have a harder time holding jobs, staying married, raising children, and even staying out of jail.

Many people believe that children are good at bouncing back and, left alone, will grow up okay. In my experience, it is true that kids can be remarkably resilient, but it's wrong to assume that they can 'grow out' of their psychiatric disorders and go on to fulfill their potential, without help. Many children with ADHD, and other conditions, find their problems compounding as they get older and responsibilities increase. Children with untreated ADHD often become adults with untreated ADHD, and with that comes a whole host of adult-sized problems (as mentioned above).

It doesn't have to be this way, though! One good example is that of Kate (not her real name), one of my clients of several years ago. Kate first came to see me in Year 10, concerned about the likelihood of failing the year. Her parents reported that Kate's teachers had often commented that she did not pay attention and often daydreamed during class. Her grades had been on a gradual decline since she started high school, and socially they felt that she was isolating herself more and more.

After screening, and a thorough assessment by her Paediatrician, Kate was diagnosed with ADHD, and prescribed Ritalin. Kate's parents chose a multidisciplinary treatment approach which included parent training, medication and counselling. With this treatment plan, Kate went from a student who was failing, to achieving all 'Bs'. Kate's parents reported that they had always known Kate was smart, but troubled. ADHD had often crossed their minds but because of the 'myths' that still exist around ADHD and stimulants they were reluctant to pursue a diagnosis. However, they said that Kate, on her very first day on medication, had come home after school and said that for the first time she actually heard what the teacher had said. Her parents showed regret for not having sought a diagnosis earlier, and felt a sense of responsibility for the gaps in Kate's learning.

Kate's story is one of hope – even though she was already in her teens when she was diagnosed, she got the help that she needed, in her childhood years, when it is most effective.

In one of the sessions, Kate reported that since treatment, her school life had become much better. She had joined the debate team where she was known for her persuasiveness and creativity. During our last session she told me that she wanted to be a 'special needs' teacher, and I know her future will be bright.

"All the risk of ADHD thus far, has been associated with not treating the condition with education, not with medication treatment itself."

– William Dodson, M.D

Take Away: **We know that many psychiatric disorders are treated more easily in childhood, giving us a window of opportunity to drastically change the lives of young people like Kate. With responsible treatment, children can learn to control their impulsivity, do well in school and have better relationships with peers and families.**

> *The truth is, there is no such thing as "normal", there are just a series of spectrums on which we all fall and how "normal" we are is largely determined by how well our strengths and weaknesses match the social norms of the times we live in.*
>
> R. Boyce

CHAPTER SEVEN

ADHD – Gadgets and Screen Time

Tristan arrived at three o'clock on the dot, looking sad. He put his school bag on the floor and took a deep sigh. "You know what, Xavier? I am going to miss these meetings," he said, rubbing his face and slumping down on the sofa.

Xavier: We still have next Friday, and remember that I'm not leaving the school for another two terms, so you can always drop in, if you like.

Tris: What will happen when you leave at the end of the year? Who will take over this room?

Xavier: All I know at this stage is that someone will be available. Not quite sure who it will be. The school Chaplin is still interviewing possible candidates. Who knows? Maybe in a couple of years you'll be sitting in this chair.

Tris: In your dreams!

Xavier: You never know! It happened to me!

Tris: One more thing before we start on the tips and strategies, do you also like computer games and watching television? Mum thinks I'm addicted to technology. She finds it hard to understand why I can concentrate when playing games, but not when doing schoolwork.

Xavier: Technology was the biggest issue between my dad and me. He couldn't understand why I could play games for hours, but not manage to do homework for fifteen minutes! I did – and still do – like gaming, but my mum and I came up with a schedule that builds in time for homework, and other activities, as well as gaming. I have learned that when you plan and prioritise, you can do a lot in a day.

Tris: I think that I waste a lot of time. I'm always late with schoolwork and never finish tests on time. I was a good soccer player until I stopped a year ago. I'd like to start playing again, but I don't know where I would have the time! I struggle with so many things!

Xavier: I'm confident that you're going to benefit from going to a paediatrician and counselling. With the correct support you'll quickly realise that there are a lot of things you can do for yourself with the support of your mum and the school. What do you struggle with the most?

Tris: I can't pin-point it exactly, but I do know that I'm disorganised, forgetful, impulsive, don't really understand time, get distracted, procrastinate and become angry very quickly.

Xavier: I can understand why you may feel overwhelmed at times and may even want to give up trying. I certainly did at times. But once I learned to plan, prioritise, schedule and follow the plan through, I felt more in control of my time and less anxious.

Tris: My procrastination is very bad. I keep on putting things off until the last minute and then I feel disappointed when I don't get a good grade.

Xavier: Because your main struggles are very similar to mine, the strategies that I learned from Joy might be beneficial for you as well. I'll make sure that

I include as many tips as possible that I got from Joy. Just remember that although we may have similar struggles, you may need to tweak my strategies in order to suit your way of learning style.

Tris: I'm excited to learn about time management. I think that's where I need to start. I suppose if I can manage time, many of my other problems will get better.

Xavier: It's often the case. If you have any additional questions, bring them along next Friday. I will have all the information ready for your Toolbox. I will come to school by bike so that we can finish at 4 pm.

FACT: In the US, 4 million children have been diagnosed with ADHD, making it the most common childhood behavioural condition. In fact, according to new data from the Centers for Disease Control and Prevention, over the past decade, the number of kids diagnosed with the disorder increased by over 50%. And in the past year, that rate has jumped by about 15%.

According to a report by the Kaiser Family Foundation, the rise in ADHD has coincided with the rise of mobile devices. Children spend, on average, seven and a half hours each day staring at screens. That's up 20% from just five years ago. Does this mean there is a positive relationship between the two? Perhaps, but it's not so clear-cut.

Imagine the following: JP sits with his parents in a restaurant, playing *Minecraft*. His head is down, his attention captivated, his eyes glued to the screen – he looks like every other child. But as he plays with his mum's iPad, his mind is processing information much differently than the other children running around the room.

If you could scan JP's brain, you'd see it's working harder, trying to absorb the bombardment of information and sensations. That increased brain activity makes it harder for him to focus on one task and control his impulses — hallmark signs of inattention. In fact, his ability to stay focused on the screen, and not anywhere else, is a characteristic of ADHD.

When he plays with gadgets, it looks like concentration, but it's not – at least not in the way we think of it. Christopher Lucas, Associate Professor of Child Psychiatry, says that children focus on video games and television in a different way than the attention they'll use to thrive in school and life. He says, "It's not sustained attention in the absence of rewards. It's sustained attention with frequent intermittent rewards."

When children play games and rack up points, move to higher levels and unlock characters and goodies, their brain is rewarded by one thing: dopamine, a neurotransmitter that's released each time they 'win', says Lucas. Dopamine is the chemical at the centre of ADHD and their love affair with electronics. Some experts even believe children seek out those screens because they have problems with their dopamine systems. In fact, medication, like

Ritalin, controls ADHD by increasing dopamine activity. So, when JP plays *Minecraft*, it's as if he's self-medicating, giving his brain that extra boost that his internal circuitry doesn't offer.

That's also why separating JP from excessive use of his iPad isn't easy. Children with ADHD are usually ridiculed and ostracised, and that isolation sends them back to those gadgets. Since electronics are likely their only consistent companion, they often develop an emotional dependency that extends beyond dopamine.

In the restaurant scenario, JP is utterly focused on the iPad, keeping constant eye contact with the screen. But without it, or his computer or portable gaming console, he's a handful. It's far easier for him to find solace in screens. They don't reject him, and they give him a place to become a different person.

"These children can also create false identities about themselves that are more positive than is realistic and thus make virtual friends online easier than in person," says Russell Barkley, a Clinical Professor of Psychiatry and Pediatrics. JP would benefit from taking an electronic 'time out', but ironically he can't pull himself away.

Like JP, many children have trouble managing screen time and knowing when to unplug. When you have ADHD, it makes it even harder to make good decisions about the use of technology. Common trouble domains include:

Time management: ADHD can make it hard to keep track of time. Hours and hours can be wasted in front of a screen.

Impulse control: Children with ADHD may be more likely to engage in risky online behaviour, like watching inappropriate videos or sexting.

Sleep: Winding down at bedtime can be challenging for children with ADHD. Screen time can make it even more difficult.

Inattention: Children with ADHD can get 'lost' in a game and forget that they have tasks that need to be done.

Distractibility: All the additional bells and whistles that gaming provides make it even more challenging for kids with ADHD to stay focused.

Social Skills: Increased screen time may mean less time to practise understanding social cues during face to face interactions.

"I think to take digital play away from these kids is to do them a disservice."

— Dr. Randy Kulman

Take Away: Recognise the potential for Internet addiction among kids with ADHD. Video games and technology are activities that may lead to addictive behaviour.

Discourage random channel surfing in favour of informed viewing. Sit down with a TV schedule, and decide what to watch, based on a show's topic and the program description. Then, structure these show times into your diary. Like much in life, it is all about balance.

CHAPTER EIGHT

Toolbox
(Tips and Strategies for the Management of ADHD)

Today is the last day of Tristan's and my formal time together. Tristan is sad and tells me that Fridays are not going to be the same – ever! He also tells me that his appointment with the paediatrician has been confirmed for the following Friday. I encourage Tristan to drop by in two weeks' time to tell me about his experience with the paediatrician and the outcome of the evaluation.

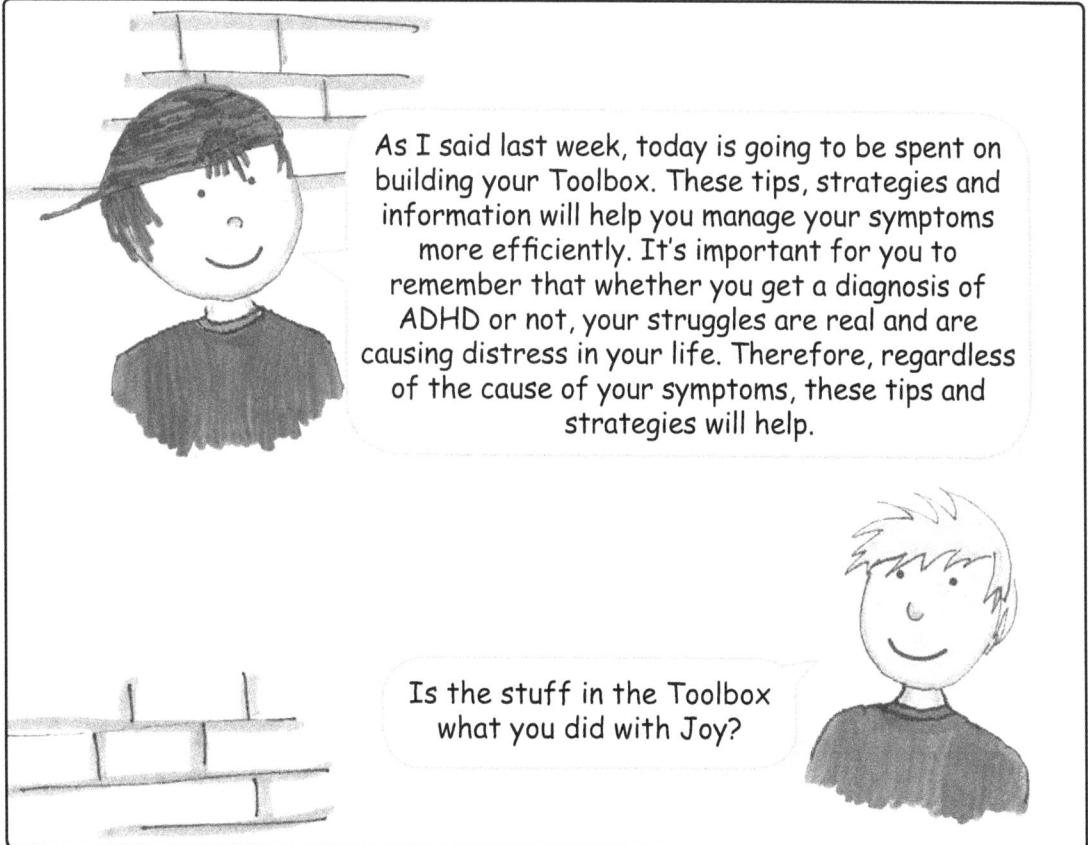

As I said last week, today is going to be spent on building your Toolbox. These tips, strategies and information will help you manage your symptoms more efficiently. It's important for you to remember that whether you get a diagnosis of ADHD or not, your struggles are real and are causing distress in your life. Therefore, regardless of the cause of your symptoms, these tips and strategies will help.

Is the stuff in the Toolbox what you did with Joy?

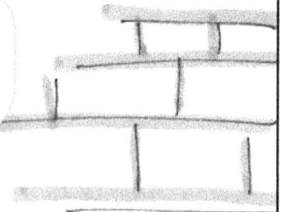

Toolbox Tip No 1
Quick Overview:
Solutions to ADHD Challenges

Although there's no cure for ADHD, many people find that—with practice and hard work—they can manage their symptoms very effectively. A diagnosis of ADHD doesn't mean that you can't be a good student or have a successful career. However, your path to achieving these goals might be different to others.

Listed below are brief solutions to challenges that people with ADHD often face. Use this tool as a starting point to think about areas where you would like to grow, and to begin generating solutions to problems.

Create Structure: More than just about anything else, the symptoms of ADHD can be managed by structure and routine. Without structure, the obligations of a single day can become overwhelming, or simply forgotten. A steady routine will help you focus on one thing at a time, with less room for distraction.

Set aside a time for everything. Try to eat, sleep, work, and relax at roughly the same time every day. This will help you follow through with each of your daily tasks. It might be a struggle to keep your routine at first, but with time you'll fall into a groove and it'll become second nature.

- Don't be overambitious — a realistic routine is better than a 'perfect' one. For example, a few blocks of 30-minute study sessions will be more productive than one overwhelming 3-hour session.

- Prioritise big 'anchor' tasks, such as sleep, meals and work. The rest of your day will revolve around these. Attach smaller tasks to your anchors. For example: "I will go for a walk right after dinner."

- A lot of people worry that a structured day will be boring. The truth is, it's only boring if you make it that way. Work fun activities into your routine, and set aside free time so you can still be spontaneous.

- Especially when you're getting started, write things down, and set alarms. Remember to set reminders a few minutes early so you have time to prepare for each task.

Example Schedule

6.30am	12pm	4pm	6pm	7pm	8pm	9.30pm
Wake up/ get ready for school	Lunch	Homework (Mon-Fri)	Dinner	Study/review for 30 minutes	Relax/ have fun/ play games/ shower	Sleep (Lights out)

Set Aside Time for Relationships: Sometimes, the symptoms of ADHD can make a person come across as indifferent and uncaring in their relationships, even when that's not the case. Whatever your challenges, setting aside time for your relationships with parents, siblings and friends can help.

Don't forget to maintain your relationships with those you don't see every day.

Stay Organised: Clutter is the enemy of ADHD. As you move from task to task, half-finished projects will start to take over your physical and mental space. This leads to distraction, and a higher probability that things will be lost or forgotten.

- **Create 'to do' lists.** Start with the quickest and easiest tasks (unless there's something urgent) so you can see immediate progress.

- **Routine.** Develop routines and stick to them

- **Keep your workspace clean.** Clear your desk of everything, except for the task you're currently working on. Additionally, give yourself five minutes at the end of each day to tidy up.

- **Downsize.** Get rid of old clothes, papers, and anything else you don't need around your room. If you've been holding onto something for five years because 'you might need it someday', it's probably OK to part ways with it!

- **Do it right away.** If a task comes up that will only take 30 seconds, and you are not doing something else that's important, do it right away. Then, it's off your 'to do' list, and out of your mind forever.

Change Your Environment to Suit You: What helps you concentrate, and what derails you from your work? Some people with ADHD need a lot of action. They work better somewhere that's vibrant and loud. Others need the opposite, no sounds, no TVs, no phones—nothing but the task at hand. Figure out what works for you and create that environment.

Need noise and activity?

• Listen to music. Or a motivational podcast.

• If your room is boring, try to liven up your workspace. Add pictures of your visions and dreams, photos of people who inspire you, and anything else that will keep you stimulated.

• Schedule regular breaks to go for a walk. Set a timer during your break so you know when to get back to work.

Need peace and quiet?

• If you live in a noisy household, use headphones to listen to 'white noise', or non-intrusive music; or earplugs to cancel out outside noises

• Designate a workspace in your home, even if it's just a corner, and remove all distractions.

• Make a habit of not having unnecessary technology at your disposal when doing homework or studying. Limit all those tempting distractions that tend to pop up when you're working.

Lifestyle: Exercise, nutrition, and sleep. Without these, you'll have a hard time taking control of your ADHD, regardless of what other steps you take. Even someone without ADHD will become restless without exercise, and distracted without food or sleep. The negative effects are only magnified by ADHD.

Find a form of exercise you enjoy. Even a 30-minute walk can have a positive impact on your health. Exercise earlier in the day can help you feel more energetic and awake throughout the day. Sports are a great outlet. Try to bring balance into your life between your social, academic and physical well-being.

When it comes to sleep, everyone's different. Eight hours a night is usually sufficient, but some people do require more. Get into a steady sleep routine, by sticking to the same bedtime and wake-up time every day, even on weekends. If sleeping issues become a problem, speak to your doctor about it.

Our knowledge about what foods help to curb the symptoms of ADHD is less clear, but many believe a diet that's high in protein, and low in sugar, can help. Nonetheless, it's important to make sure you eat several well-balanced meals every day. If you feel hungry between meals, aim to have healthy snacks that include fruit, dairy (or dairy alternatives), wholegrain products and lean protein such as fish and eggs. Planned meals double as a great way to stay in a routine.

Toolbox Tip No 2
Problem-Solving

Xavier: How are you at problem-solving?

Tris: Pretty bad I, think! Actually, it's annoying because on some things I can manage OK! But making decisions on stuff is very difficult.

Xavier: I so agree with you! When it comes to my personal life, I am useless – well was useless! Now I just use the step process that Joy taught me and somehow it just makes it so much easier.

Tris: I like to do things in steps!

Xavier: The step process 'template' that I have included in your Toolbox is very easy to use and it works for pretty much everything. The good thing about it is that after a while you'll find that it becomes an automatic process. For bigger decisions, I still prefer to write it down though!

Individuals with ADHD need to learn to recognise when they are experiencing difficulty completing a task or are becoming overwhelmed and cannot figure out where and how to start. If they don't, it can lead to procrastination and avoidance. Mastering the skills of problem-solving helps individuals understand how to analyse and talk their way through a problem, rather than resorting to avoidance or verbal and physical aggression.

Safren et. al., (2005) suggests the following steps when problem-solving:

- Define the problem
- Brainstorm solutions

- Discuss pros and cons
- Decide and plan
- Implement
- Review / revise

Writing out your problem will help to organise information, see it from new angles, and identify the most important issues. Below is the step process to problem-solving:

1. Define your problem: Be as clear and comprehensive as possible. If there are many parts to your problem, describe each of them. Examples might be, "I cannot decide whether to go to college or take a gap year." Or, "I cannot decide what to do about a co-worker who's giving me a hard time."

TIP: If you find it difficult to separate your emotions from the problem, try to complete this step from the perspective of an impartial friend.

2. List all possible solutions: Come up with as many solutions as possible, regardless of how 'do-able' they are, what the consequences may be, or whether or not they sound outrageous. We often get stuck on what worked in the past, or the first idea that comes to mind. There are usually many solutions to a problem, and our first ideas aren't always the best.

3. Assess the pros and cons of each solution: Begin by throwing out any solutions that are obviously ineffective or impractical. Next, look at your remaining solutions, and determine which ones are the most likely to be successful by identifying them in-depth. This can be done by examining the strengths and weaknesses of each solution. During this stage, you might come up with new solutions, or find that a combination of multiple solutions is better than any one idea.

TIP: If you're having a hard time thinking of pros and cons for each solution, ask yourself these questions:

- Is this a short-term or long-term solution?
- How likely am I to follow through with this solution?
- How will this solution affect other people?

4. Rate each solution: Rate the pros and cons of each solution on a scale of one to ten as objectively as possible.

5. Implement the best solution: Now that you've rated each option, look at the one that is rated the highest. Determine whether this is really the one you want to pick. If 'yes', implement it.

6. Evaluate the outcome: Evaluate the effectiveness of the plan. Decide whether the existing plan needs to be revised, or whether a new plan is needed to better address the problem. If you are not pleased with the outcome, return to step 2 to select a new option or revise the existing plan, and repeat the remaining steps.

Remember, this problem-solving strategy can help you deal with difficult situations, but it needs some practice. So, next time you find yourself worrying about a real problem that is in the here-and-now and you have some control over, choose not to worry about it immediately. Postpone it until you can sit down with a piece of paper and try problem-solving during your thinking time. It is more productive than worrying, it will reduce your anxiety, and by the end of it you should have a plan of action. Follow this simple template:

Problem Solving Template

Background	Problem-Solving/Decision-Making Principles		
	Identify Central issue/problem:		
	Explore:		
	Solution 1:	Solution 2:	Solution 3:
	Advantages:	Advantages:	Advantages:
	Disadvantages:	Disadvantages:	Disadvantages:
	Choose your option:		
	Act upon your choice:		
	Evaluate: (Ask the following questions) In what ways was your solution effective? In what ways was your solution not effective? If you could go back in time, what would you change about how you handled the problem? What advice would you give to someone else who was dealing with the same problem?		

Toolbox Tip No 3
Mindfulness

Xavier: Remember we spoke about 'mindfulness'? Using breathing techniques to help you manage your anger? That is your next tool. Mindfulness occurs when we pay attention to what is happening in the 'here and now'. We observe our emotions, our thoughts, our surroundings, without passing judgement. We apply this same focus of attention to situations both good and bad. Fear and anger can hit us unexpectedly and when we do not have a prior plan for dealing with these feelings, we can be thrown off balance and react badly.

Tris: But I do breathe already!

Xavier: You're quite right, we all breathe, Tris, but we need to learn to breathe in a special way. Joy used the analogy of a 'monkey brain'. She gave examples of how I could be sitting in classroom, but my mind would be elsewhere; playing games, or thinking of the weekend, only realising that I had been miles away when the teacher asked me a question and I couldn't answer! It's all about paying attention to the 'NOW'.

Tris: The 'monkey brain' happens to me often! Is it hard to do the breathing stuff?

Xavier: Not so much 'hard', but it needs quite a lot of practice. In your Toolbox, you will find easy exercises for you to practise. I know that there are mindfulness apps that you can download to your phone. Ask your mum about them.

Tris: Is it like music and stuff?

Xavier: Yes, there is relaxing music too. School kids can really benefit from this technique. Studies show that kids who practise mindfulness concentrate and perform better in exams.

Unlike many tools for ADHD, mindfulness develops the individual's inner skills. It teaches you to pay attention to paying attention, and can also make people more aware of their emotional state, so they won't react impulsively – a real problem for people with ADHD.

Given that you have to breathe, why not use this free, highly-portable alternative treatment to manage your ADHD symptoms?

Researchers have talked about using mindfulness for ADHD for some time, but the question was always whether people with ADHD could really do it, especially if hyperactivity was present. Now we know that deep breathing can balance the autonomic nervous system, which helps individuals with ADHD become more attentive and relaxed.

Your Autonomic Nervous System (ANS) has two components: a stress response and a recharge response. Children with ADHD have nervous systems that are out of whack: most of the time the stress and recharge responses are under-active. But when the stress response kicks in for an individual with ADHD, it goes into high gear, compared to those who don't have the condition. For your brain to work better, and for you to be less impulsive and hyperactive, both components of the ANS need to work optimally, and in the right balance. Deep breathing can help accomplish these goals.

According to Richard Brown, M.D., Associate Clinical Professor of Psychiatry, "Amazing things happen in the body and brain when we slow down our breathing to five or six full breaths a minute. The heart, lungs, and blood vessels work more efficiently, delivering more oxygen to the body's tissues and the brain. Parts of the brain that deal with complex problems begin to function better. People with ADHD feel a lot calmer, are better able to make good judgments, and are less easily frustrated."

What's in it for you?

Teens may see mindfulness as completely unrelated to their busy lives. But there are many ways that adolescents and adults alike can benefit from a mindfulness practice. Studies have shown that:

- students who practise mindfulness before an exam perform better than students who do not;
- mindfulness helps improve performance on standardised tests;
- mindfulness can improve concentration;
- mindfulness can help with anxiety, stress, depression and emotional regulation (conditions that often co-exist with ADHD).

Breathing Techniques

Deep Breathing: Find a quiet place to sit where you won't be interrupted. Close your eyes, relax your eyes, neck, hands, and feet, and complete five or six full breaths in a minute, keeping your awareness on the breath moving inside of you. Listening to soft music, as you do breathing and muscle relaxation exercises also helps. Practise:

1. Breathe in slowly. Count in your head and make sure the inward breath lasts at least five seconds. Pay attention to the feeling of the air filling your lungs.

2. Hold your breath for five to ten seconds (again, keep count). You don't want to feel uncomfortable, but it should last quite a bit longer than an ordinary breath.

3. Breathe out very slowly for five to ten seconds (count!). Pretend you're breathing through a straw to slow yourself down. Try using a real straw to practise.

4. Repeat the breathing process until you feel calm.

Imagery

Think about some of your favourite and least favourite places. If you think about the place hard enough – if you really try to think about what it's like – you may begin to have feelings you associate with that location. Our brain has the ability to create emotional reactions based entirely on our thoughts. The imagery technique uses this to its advantage.

Make sure you're somewhere quiet without too much noise or distraction. You'll need a few minutes to just spend quietly, in your mind. Think of a place that's calming for you. Some examples are the beach, hiking on a mountain, relaxing at home with a friend, or playing with a pet.

Paint a picture of the calming place in your mind. Don't just think of the place briefly, imagine every little detail. Go through each of your senses and imagine what you would experience in your relaxing place. Here's an example using a beach:

- **Sight:** The sun is high in the sky and you're surrounded by white sand. There's no one else around. The water is a greenish-blue and waves are calmly rolling in from the ocean.

- **Sound:** You can hear the deep pounding and splashing of the waves. There are squawking seagulls somewhere in the background.

- **Touch:** The sun is warm on your back, but a breeze cools you down just enough to be comfortable. You can feel sand moving between your toes.

- **Taste:** You have a glass of lemonade that's sweet and refreshing.

- **Smell:** You can smell the fresh ocean air, full of salt and calming aromas.

Progressive Muscle Relaxation

The 'fight-or-flight' response (see below) is a primitive, automatic, inborn response that prepares the body to "fight" or "flee" from perceived attack, threat or harm to our survival. Increased tension in our muscles during this response can lead to a feeling of stiffness, or even back and neck pain. Progressive muscle relaxation teaches us to become more aware of this tension so we can better identify and address stress.

The idea of this technique is to intentionally tense each muscle, and then to release the tension. Practise the following exercise:

Find a private and quiet location. You should sit or lie down somewhere comfortable. Starting with your feet:

a. Tense the muscles in your toes by curling them into your foot. Notice how it feels when your foot is tense. Hold the tension for five seconds.

b. Release the tension from your toes. Let them relax. Notice how your toes feel differently after you release the tension.

c. Tense the muscles all throughout your calf. Hold it for five seconds. Notice how the feeling of tension in your leg feels.

d. Release the tension from your calf, and notice the feeling of relaxation.

Follow this pattern of tensing and releasing tension all throughout your body. After you finish with your feet and legs, move up through your torso, arms, hands, neck and head.

The 'Fight-or-Flight' responses

The 'fight-or-flight' response is one of the tools your body uses to protect you from danger. When you feel threatened, the 'fight-or-flight' response is automatically triggered, and several physiological changes prepare you to either confront or flee from the threat:

1. Symptoms of Fight or Flight

- Increased heart rate
- Racing thoughts
- Difficulty concentrating
- Dizziness or light-headedness
- Shaking
- Nausea / 'butterflies in the stomach'
- Rapid, shallow breathing
- Sweating
- Tensed Muscles

2. How is the 'fight-or-flight' response triggered?

Even threats to emotional well-being, such as the fear of embarrassment before giving a presentation, can trigger the 'fight-or-flight' response. In these cases, the symptoms often do more harm than good. An increased heart rate and sweating might help you escape from a bear, but they won't do much to help you look cool and collected during a presentation.

3. Is the 'fight-or-flight' response bad?

Everyone will experience the 'fight-or-flight' response at times, to varying degrees. Usually, it's natural, healthy, and not a problem. However, when the 'fight-or-flight' response leads to excessive anger, anxiety, prolonged stress, or other problems, it might be time to intervene.

4. How can I manage the 'fight-or-flight' response?

In addition to the 'fight-or-flight' response, your body can also initiate an opposing relaxation response. Many symptoms of the relaxation response counteract 'fight-or-flight', such as slower and deeper breathing, relaxed muscles, and a slower heart rate. The relaxation response can be triggered by using relaxation skills, such as deep breathing or progressive muscle relaxation.

Practise coherent breathing when you're calm. A lot of people say, "Oh, I'll do it when I get stressed." That's like waiting for the storm to hit and then taking precautions, often too late! When you get upset with your teacher, or when you lose your lunch money, you'll have a head start at getting yourself calm and focused, if you've practised. The technique becomes an almost automatic response when you find yourself in stressful situations.

"Be where you are, otherwise you will miss your life."

— Buddha

Toolbox Tip No 4
Time Management and ADHD

Xavier: Time management is a biggie. Most of us with ADHD have a very poor sense of time. We also have trouble estimating time. For example, guessing how long it is going to take to complete an assignment. How good are you at using time, Tris?

Tris: Well, I'm very good at wasting time. I'm always rushing around at the last minute trying to finish homework – sometimes even doing it in the car on my way to school. Even getting ready in the mornings is a real struggle! A few times mum had to leave for work and I had to find my way to school, otherwise she would have been late.

Xavier: Tell me about it! My dad often left me behind, but luckily we don't live very far from school, so I could just use my bike – not nice in winter, though!

Tris: We live far from school, so biking is not an option for me.

Xavier: As I said, time management is a real concern and one that I still struggle with at times. The most important thing is to realise that you need guidance and support, and be open to use strategies in the environment that makes time more visible for you. For example, use a wristwatch with an alarm beeper to remind you when to start or switch a task, practise time estimation – write down how long it actually takes to complete your homework, and go to bed on time. My mum wakes me up thirty minutes earlier than is necessary, so I can take my medication and it has time to kick in. Then, when I do get up, I'm more alert and can get ready in no time at all.

According to Russell Barkley, acquiring a sense of time is a developmental skill that is significantly delayed in students with ADHD. Barkley points out that time is the enemy of everyone with ADHD. According to him, an event must enter the person's 'window on time' (limited duration during which something can be accomplished before the need to take action is felt). Individuals with ADHD also have trouble estimating time. For example, guessing how long a task will take. They may feel overwhelmed by a homework task because they have no sense of how long it will take to complete, nor where or how to get started. They also don't plan ahead and instead put off projects until the night before they're due.

These individuals live in the 'here and now'. It's as though everything is today; there is no tomorrow. An impaired sense of time is a lifelong problem for individuals with ADHD that shows only limited improvement, even with medication, thus helping students learn compensatory skills is vital. Punishing time-related behaviours in ADHD individuals by sending them to detention or penalising grades is not especially effective in changing behaviour. Punishment can at times provoke more anxiety and even poorer school performance. An impaired sense of time contributes to the following problems (Zeigler Dendy, Chris A. 2011):

- Tardiness

- Avoidance of homework assignments

- Late completion of class assignments

- Inability to estimate how long a task will take

- Not allowing enough time to complete work

- Not planning ahead for the completion of major class projects

- Delayed start on projects

Practical Tips to Manage Time:

- **Use a 'to do' list or diary:** Writing down your responsibilities has a number of benefits. Not only will it ensure you don't forget anything, it also reduces stress by allowing you to drop your mental checklist.

- **Prioritise your tasks:** Focus on completing the most important, and the quickest tasks, first. If you have a few 'to do' tasks that will only take five minutes, knock them out quickly for the peace of mind.

- **Break large tasks into smaller pieces:** It's easy to feel overwhelmed when you have a really big task ahead of you. Breaking big tasks into small pieces will help you get started, which is often the hardest part. For example, writing a paper can be 'chunked down', such as doing research, preparing an outline, and writing an introductory paragraph.

- **Limit distractions:** Spend a few days recording how much time you spend on distractions, such as social media or TV. Then, cut out the distractions you don't actually enjoy, and schedule time for the ones you do enjoy. Always set an alarm so you know when to get back to work.

- **If you can't limit your distractions, get away from them:** If you know that you will succumb to distractions, get away from them. Create clear boundaries between work and play by putting up a 'Do Not Disturb' sign on your door, turning off your phone, or going to a coffee shop that doesn't have a TV. Everyone is different in this regard—make the changes you need to, so you can focus.

- **Give yourself time between tasks:** Plan on arriving fifteen minutes early to appointments, and bring something to do in case you find yourself waiting. Scheduling some buffer time will help to reduce your stress when things inevitably happen

- **Let yourself be 'less than perfect':** If you try to complete every task to perfection, some of your other responsibilities won't get done at all. Focus on completing everything to an acceptable level, and then go back to improve upon your work, if you have time.

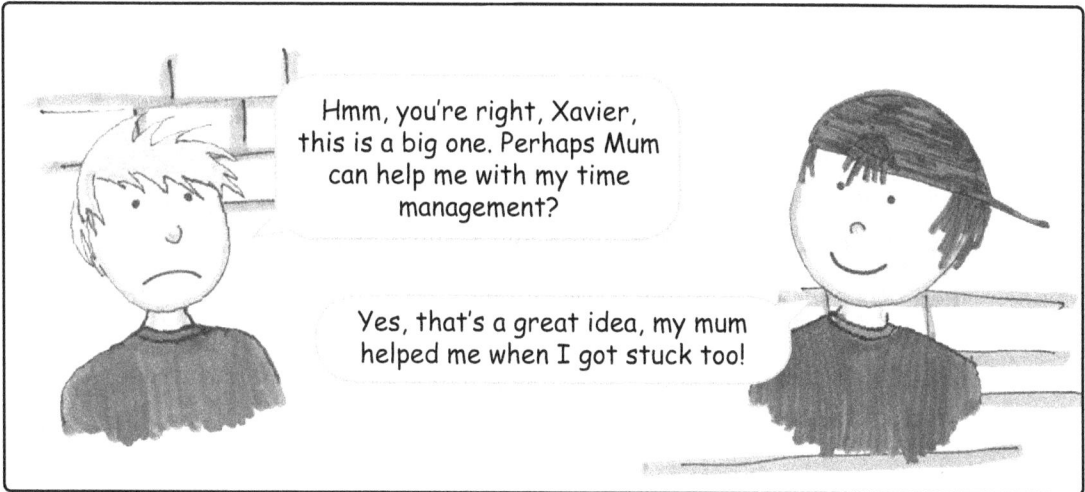

Toolbox Tip No 5
Anger Management

Xavier: My dad often told me that I was so stubborn that I'd argue with a fence post! Yelling battles with my parents were common. Of all the emotions, this was the one that caused the most issues in my family.

Tris: Yeah, 'short fuses' get me into trouble a lot. I get angry and frustrated and then have a big blow up. These blow ups have cost me friends. I have a hard time controlling my anger. Stuff builds up inside me, then I erupt like a volcano.

Xavier: Many kids with ADHD struggle with managing their anger. Experts believe that of all the emotions, anger is the one that causes the most problems for children with ADHD.

Tris: Yeah! I can see why they would say that. I don't fight and stuff, but I get angry with adults and with friends when I feel left out, teased or treated unfairly, like when Mrs Smart kept me back after school a couple of weeks ago.

Xavier: Imagine a day that goes like this: You arrive at school without your homework and the teacher wants to know why. Later, you can't remember the instructions the teacher gave you for your worksheet, so you don't complete it. At lunch, you get picked on by some kids that you don't even know. And during the last period of the day, you get called out for speaking out of turn.

Now, you get home and face more tasks, which means more things that might go wrong. You already had a stressful day, but your parents don't know that. You are told to make your bed, because you forgot to make in the morning, and to tidy up your room that is starting to look like a pigsty. Instead of taking it in your stride, you become overwhelmed and the volcano erupts.

Tris: Omigosh, have you got a camera inside my house? That is my life!

Xavier: No, Tris! – I know it so well because that was my life four years ago! But not as bad anymore. Joy helped me understand the 'anger cycle' and to identify my 'anger warnings'. As I said last week, I do still get angry and that's normal, but this knowledge, together with practising mindfulness and problem-solving skills, have really helped me to be more in control of my anger.

Tris: I've never told anyone before, but I think that dad left because of me. He couldn't handle my temper tantrums. When he belted me, mum would get upset and they would fight. I really need to get my anger under control!

Xavier: It must be difficult for you to think that your dad left because of your temper tantrums! I suggest that if you go and see Joy or any other psychologist that you speak to him/her about those feelings. I spoke to Joy about my complicated relationship with my dad and his lack of understanding of my challenges and it really helped me.

Some children have difficulty controlling their emotions when they are frustrated or upset. For a child who has ADHD, the problems are usually externalised. Hence, they are more noticeable. For example, you may talk back, have a temper, refuse to follow rules and occasionally get into fights at school. Consequently, you may have yelling battles with your parents. These characteristics may also irritate your friends who may, over time, not want to spend time with you. Emotional issues, such as friendship break ups, can be earth-shattering and may cause you to react impulsively and later regret your actions.

It is also important to look for signs of other problems that might be masked by anger. For example, aggression can mask depression in children. Generally, if you are passing at school and family life is good, it's a lot easier to control your emotions. One client reported, "It is hard for me to exercise control over what I say to my mum, especially when she picks me up from school, when I'm worn out after trying so hard to keep myself under control in class all day. I think that mum understands how hard it can be when you have ADHD and she doesn't take it personally. I feel bad, though".

Anger Cycle

TRIGGERING EVENTS

THOUGHTS - eg "It's not fair"

EMOTIONS - eg Anger, frustration, guilt

PHYSICAL AROUSAL - eg Racing heart, shaking

BEHAVIOUR RESPONSES - eg Fighting, avoiding

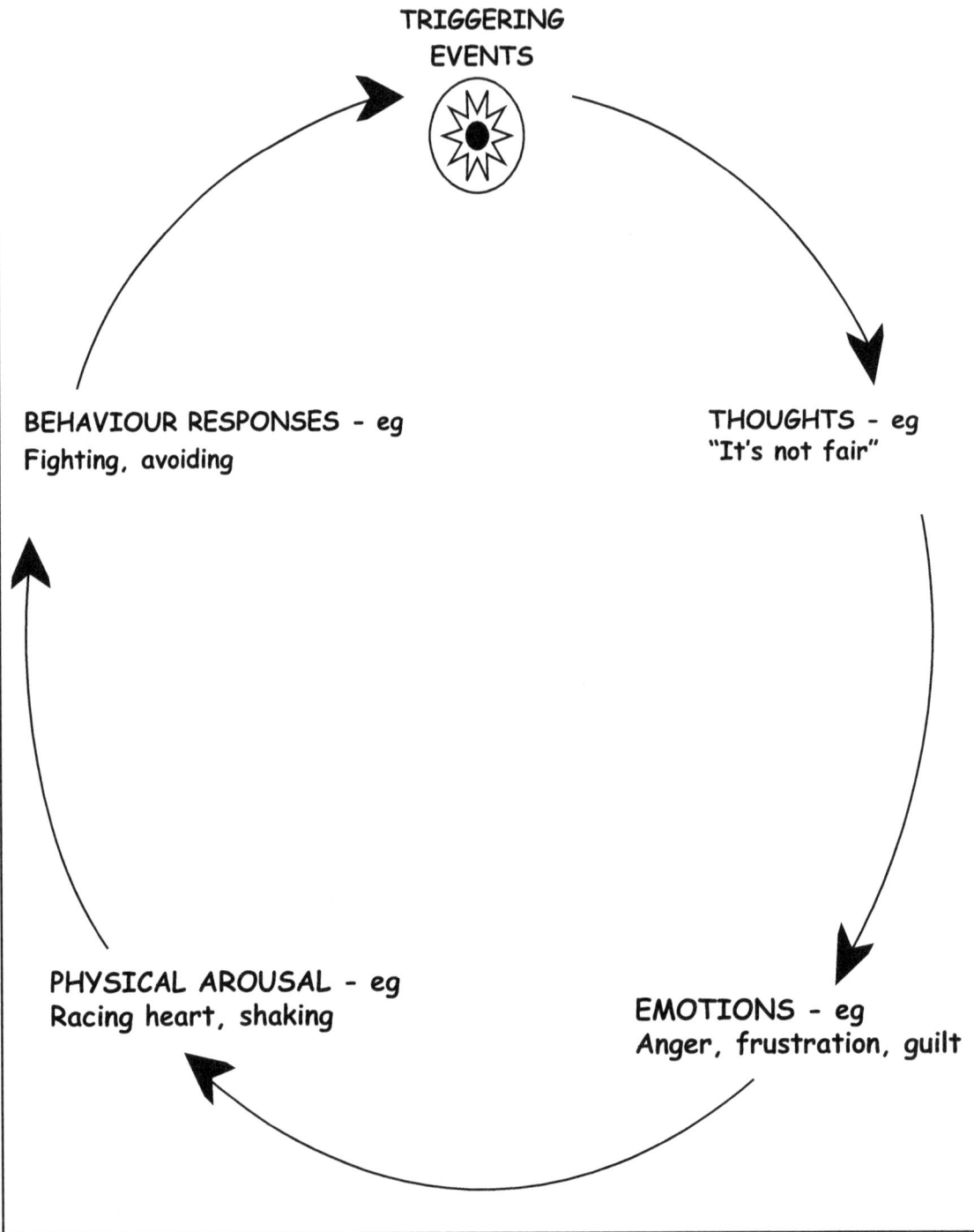

Adapted from TherapistAid.com

1. Triggering event: An event or situation 'triggers' a person's anger. Examples:

- Getting told off while gaming

- Having a bad day at school

- Feeling disrespected

2. Negative thoughts: Irrational and negative thoughts occur as a result of the triggering event. Examples:

- "I am the worst child ever."

- "The teachers don't like me; that is why they always pick on me."

3. Emotional Response: Negative thoughts lead to negative emotions, even if the thoughts are irrational. Examples:

- Feelings of shame and guilt due to being the 'worst child ever'.

- Rage directed toward a teacher.

4. Physical Symptoms: The body automatically responds to anger with several symptoms. Examples:

- Racing heart

- Clenched fists

- Sweating

- Shaking

5. Behavioural responses: The person reacts based upon thoughts, feelings and physical symptoms. Examples:

- Fighting

- Yelling

- Arguing

- Critricising

- Avoiding

Awareness of Anger Warning signs

Sometimes anger can affect what you say or do before you even recognise how you're feeling. You may become so used to the feeling of anger that you don't notice it; sort of like how you can hear the sound on a radio, or the humming of a refrigerator, but block it from your mind.

Even if you aren't aware of your anger, it influences how you behave. The first step to managing anger is learning to recognise your anger 'warning signs' that will tip you off about how you're feeling.

How do you react when you feel angry? Some of these warning signs might start when you are only a little irritated, and others might start when you are very angry. Do the warning signs below resonate with you?

Do you recognise any of the following 'warning signs' in yourself?

Yes/ No	Warning Sign	Yes/ No	Warning Sign
	Tight muscles in neck, back or jaw		Punch walls
	Clenched teeth		Start sweating
	Saying bad words		Trembling
	Flushed face		Punching
	Upset stomach		Ruminating
	Raising voice		Go quiet, 'shut down'
	Feeling short of breath		Pace around the room
	Headaches		Throw things
	Mind goes blank		Finger pointing

Adapted from TherapistAid.com

Ways to Manage Anger

- **Recognise Your Anger Early:** Learn the warning signs that you're getting angry, so you can change the situation quickly. If you're already yelling, it's probably too late. Some common signs are feeling hot, raising voices, balling of fists, shaking and arguing.

- **Take Time Out:** Temporarily go off by yourself until you've calmed down. If other people are involved, explain to them that you need a few minutes alone to calm down. Problems usually aren't solved when one or more people are angry.

- **Deep Breathing:** Take a minute to just breathe. Breathe in slowly. Count in your head and make sure the inward breath lasts at least five seconds. Pay attention to the feeling of the air filling your lungs. Hold your breath for five to ten seconds. Breathe out very slowly for five to ten seconds (count!). Pretend you're breathing through a straw to slow yourself down. Really keep track of time, or you might cheat yourself! The counting helps take your mind off the situation as well.

- **Exercise:** Exercise serves as an emotional release. Chemicals released in your brain during the course of exercise create a sense of relaxation and happiness.

- **Express your Anger:** Once you've calmed down, express your frustration. Try to be assertive, but not confrontational. Expressing your anger will help avoid the same problems in the future.

- **Think of the Consequence:** What will be the outcome of your next anger-fueled action? Will arguing convince the other person that you're right? Will you be happier after the fight?

- **Visualisation:** Paint a picture of the calming place in your mind. Don't just think of the place briefly — imagine every little detail. Go through each of your senses and imagine what you would experience in your relaxing place. What do you see, smell, hear, feel and taste? Maybe you're on a beach with sand between your toes and waves crashing in the distance. Spend a few minutes imagining every detail of your relaxing scene.

- **Use your own Traffic Light:**

  o If you are feeling safe and calm in a situation, think GREEN: "I can stay here. It's okay for me to keep doing what I'm doing."

  o If you feel yourself getting upset about something, think YELLOW: "I should be careful here; I am starting to feel my anger warning signs. It's okay to stay for now, but if I get more upset, I'll have to remove myself from the situation. Use your breathing techniques and repeat to yourself, "I have control over my feelings. I choose".

  o If you are upset, angry or in danger, think RED; "I need to leave. I am angry now." "I need to call Mum" or "I need to call 000."

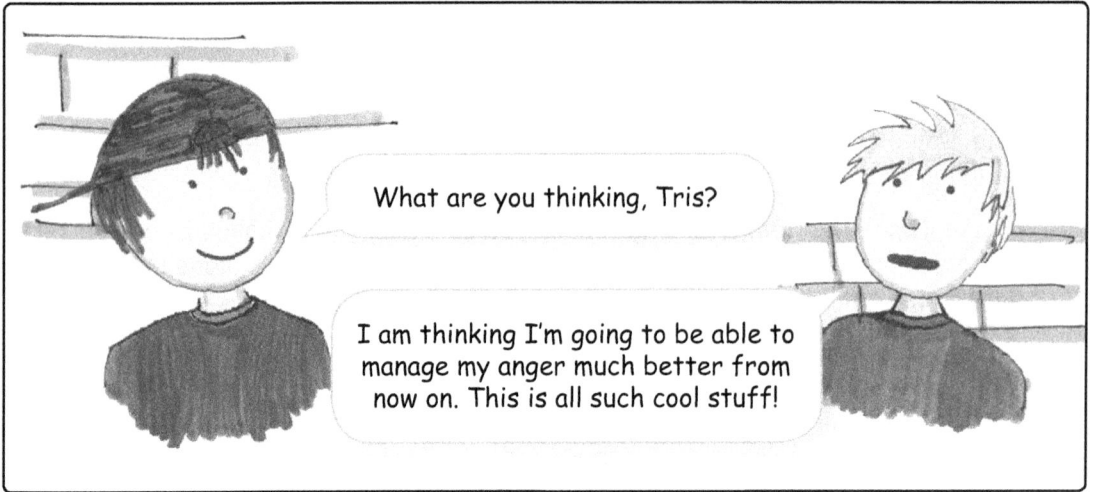

Toolbox Tip No 6
Planning and Organising

Xavier: How organised are you, mate?

Tris: I'm such a scatterbrain, I forget and lose everything. I forget to do my chores and even to hand in my completed homework. Who does that? My bedroom and backpack are a complete mess. Mum helps me, at least once a week, to organise my stuff. Otherwise I can't find anything.

Xavier: Well, you're not alone; I still misplace stuff. Yesterday Mum had to help me find my watch. It nearly made me late for school! You know where it was? Under my bed. And you know what else was under my bed? A jacket that I had been looking for, for months.

Tris: Does that mean that there is nothing that can be done about it!

Xavier: No, not at all! I am much better at planning and organising than before. The skills that Joy taught me, like the use of a diary, prioritising tasks, keeping to routine and having a launch station, really helps. Sometimes I do still slack off, which is not good.

Tris: It's so weird! Because most of the time I do know what I need to do to be organised. And when I do it, things go well, but then it all just goes bad again.

Xavier: What Joy taught me is that often it is what you say to yourself after you have lapsed (gone back to your old ways) that can either help you get back on track or lead you into relapse (go back to your old unhelpful ways). If you see your lapse as a sign of failure, you are likely to just 'give up' and go back to your old ways of doing things. If you see your lapse as a slip-up, and exercise self-compassion, then getting back on track is easier.

Most individuals with ADHD struggle with being organised. They are often thought of as 'visual organisers' – this means that they like to see where things are. "I hate putting things away because I cannot always remember where I put them," said a client. Learning to be organised requires time to set up and maintain an organisational system, but once you have an organisational system in place, it will reduce difficulties related to feeling overwhelmed or out of control and missing out on opportunities because of missed deadlines or lost schoolwork. Being organised helps reduce procrastination, impulsivity and distractibility.

Organisation is not about having all of your ducks in a row! It is about having systems that work with the way you think – ones that may appear illogical to someone else, but that are simple and easy to use and that you find appealing and interesting.

Note: There is no organisational system in the world that will work if it is not maintained. Setting up a system is only the first step, for regardless of how good a system is, it will fail without **maintenance**; **maintenance** will fail without **routine**; and **routine** will fail without **commitment** and **time**.

When creating a routine, discuss various options with a family member or someone in your circle of support. If a **routine isn't working**, brainstorm **WHY???** and explore acceptable alternatives!

Getting Organised at School: When taking control of your locker, binder, or backpack, organise contents for easy access. Start by discussing the goal, not just to have them neater, but also to:

- make it easier to find stuff
- carry only what is necessary
- have fewer hassles forgetting stuff
- spend less mental energy remembering

Two organisational principles apply: group like with like (categorise) and everything needs a home (where you can find it!).

Organising the Homework Area:

- Desk or kitchen table
- Privacy vs. working with a buddy
- Portable homework supplies container (see-through) or basket with homework

supplies that you can move around easily

- File or accordion folder for work that does not need to be in the binder, but may still be needed to study for tests/exams

- Count down timer or an alarm clock

Maintaining your organisation system:

- **Daily:** Determine a time and place to empty the bag of homework, notices, planner, and any necessary items for that day's homework.

- **Daily:** Determine a time to check that everything has been returned to the bag (including completed homework) and to put the bag in your launch station where it will be seen, and not forgotten in the morning. Add other items that need to go to school for projects, sports, music etc.

- **Weekly:** Set a time (Sunday night?) to go through the backpack to remove anything that does not belong, and make sure everything that does belong is in the bag. Do the same with the desk or other work areas. Put papers that are no longer needed (but should be saved for test review etc.) into a separate, clearly-labelled filing system (hanging folders, accordion file, desktop magazine holders).

- **Focus on Organising and not on Critiquing:** Ignore the graded or messy papers and the junk food wrappers (don't beat yourself up about it).

- **The goal is to change:** Change the 'have to' 'must do' into, "I Want To!"

Note: It may take some time in the short term to set up these systems, but it will be worth it in the long term. Try to use the strategies of problem-solving and breaking down large tasks into smaller steps, if you feel overwhelmed by the prospect of setting systems. If you take one step at a time, you will be able to complete these tasks. Continue to monitor your progress by reviewing:

- your use of the calendar and task list

- your use of the 'A,' 'B' and 'C' priority ratings

- your use of problem-solving and your ability to break a large task into manageable steps

"The secret of change is to focus all of your energy, not on fighting the old, but on building the new."

– Socrates

Toolbox Tip No 7
Procrastination

Xavier: My favourite – procrastination!

Tris: That could easily be my middle name! My mum says I do it all the time; I never start things when she tells me to. She says that I need to stop saying that I will do it tomorrow! Or that I have plenty of time to finish. She always says, "Tristan, yesterday you said you would do it today!"

Xavier: I think that most people with ADHD struggle with procrastination – in my case I can follow through on some tasks, but tasks where I fear failure or disapproval from others are the worst.

Tris: Yeah! I know what you mean! I struggle to get started on most things. I'm also scared of failure, but most times I just feel that I'm not smart enough or as good as the other kids, so I don't even try.

Xavier: Sometimes Mum says that I'm a bit of a perfectionist like my dad!

Tris: Really! Can kids with ADHD be perfectionists?

Xavier: Well, it seems like it!

Procrastination is common human behaviour that is often mistaken for 'laziness'. In everyday language people use definitions like, 'putting off', 'postponing', and 'leaving to the last minute'.

For the purpose of this book 'procrastination' is defined as: Choosing to delay or not complete a task or goal you've committed to, and instead doing something of lesser importance, despite there being negative consequences to not following through on the original task or goal. It is important to remember that everyone procrastinates. However, problematic procrastination can be distinguished from more general procrastination, by the degree of the impact that it has on your life.

Getting started for many of us is about feeling 'ready' at three levels:

- Emotionally

- Physically

- Mentally

Managing the issues of each level in advance will make it easier to actually start a task, but at times the thought of preparing to work can feel like added effort, and lead to avoidance. This belief needs to be challenged, and preparation needs to be seen as beneficial, and not a waste of time. Remember the 5Ps - Prior Preparation Prevents Poor Performance.

Emotional Level Preparation: Address the potential benefits of getting started:

- You have to do the work anyway, so stalling and postponing doesn't make it go away

- Getting started more easily means less wasted time and thus more free time

- Being able to work independently means less nagging from others (e.g., mum, dad or teachers)

- Visualise what you will do with more Free Time!

Is something else getting in the way of getting started? Ask yourself:

- Is the work reasonable?

- Is the amount of work reasonable?

- How is my Emotional Fuel Tank?

- Has procrastination been 'effective' in the past?

Physical Level Preparation: Create your own workspace that is enjoyable as well as functional:

- **Where:** Is supervision helpful/necessary?

- **Seating:** Be willing to be flexible and creative – standing desk, lap desk, ball chair, etc.

- **Visual space:** Clear and attractive, personal/private, visual representation of values and goals etc.

- **Supplies:** Computer, stationery, clock, timer, music, fidgets, water, snacks

Mental Level Preparation: Before learning can happen, you must believe that you have the ability to learn. How is your mindset?

- Do you feel confident that you have the materials and information you need?

- Do you understand the expectations?

- Do you feel that you have the ability to complete the work, or the access to the help you will need?

Planning the Time

- How much time is REALLY needed for the actual work?

- What about breaks?

- What is the benefit?

- What makes up the break time?

- Is there a benefit to planning the overall approach?

Clearing your Head

- Make sure your space is all set up

- Be mindful of negative 'poisonous' thoughts

- Set your intention: What do you want the outcome to be?

- Have a visual reminder of your goal in view

- Have a breathing technique and a mantra (I can do this; it will soon be over; this is taking me closer to my goal; I am doing this in service of my values of education and success, etc.)

Unhelpful Rules & Assumptions

One of the reasons people procrastinate is because they hold unhelpful rules and assumptions about themselves or how the world works.

These unhelpful rules and assumptions often generate some form of discomfort about doing a task or goal (e.g., anger, resentment, frustration, boredom, anxiety, fear, embarrassment, depression, despair, exhaustion, etc). Procrastination becomes a way of avoiding the discomfort of the task to be carried out.

The unhelpful rules and assumptions most often linked to procrastination are:

Needing to Be in Charge: e.g., "Things should be done my way. I shouldn't have to do things

I don't want to, or just because someone else says so";

Pleasure Seeking: e.g., "Life's too short to be doing things that are boring or hard; fun should always come first";

Fear of Failure or Disapproval: e.g., "I must do things perfectly, otherwise I will fail or others will think badly of me";

Fear of Uncertainty or Catastrophe: e.g., "I must be certain of what will happen. What if it's bad? I am better off not doing anything than risking it";

Low Self-Confidence: e.g., "I can't do it. I am just too incapable and inadequate";

Depleted Energy: e.g., "I can't do things when I am stressed, fatigued, unmotivated, or depressed".

Consequences of Procrastination

The 'positive' consequences of procrastination, such as relief from discomfort about doing the task, feeling good for having stuck to your unhelpful rules and assumptions, and gaining pleasure from your procrastination activities, are all 'pay-offs' that keep procrastination going.

The negative consequences of procrastination, such as more discomfort (e.g., guilt and shame), preserving one's unhelpful rules and assumptions, 'self-criticism', piling up tasks, punishment or loss, also keep procrastination going. All these things only serve to make the task or goal even less appealing.

The Procrastination Cycle

The Procrastination Cycle shows us that procrastination is like a vicious negative spiral that we get stuck in. The good thing about a cycle is that usually we can reverse it from a negative cycle to a more positive one. It can be helpful to have a clear plan of action for what we need to do when procrastination arises. When faced with a task or goal you would usually procrastinate over, put these steps into practie:

- Adjust your unhelpful rules and assumptions;
- Tolerate your discomfort;
- Dismiss your procrastination excuses;
- Be motivational towards yourself, rather than being critical;
- Put into action practical strategies to stop procrastinating.

It is important to realise that procrastination is a habit, and like any habit it will take time, practice, persistence and patience to change from 'procrastinator' to 'doer'. Expect to have days you feel like a 'doer', and days you feel like you have slipped back into 'procrastination mode'.

The old saying of "two steps forward, one step back" is very true. If you anticipate setbacks when you commit to changing your procrastination, when you face a bump in the road, you will be less likely to blame yourself and give up.

"When there is a hill to climb, don't think that waiting will make it smaller."

– Anonymous

I don't want to procrastinate, but sometimes I just can't help it

Don't worry mate, just be sure to look over these tips on procrastination regularly. And again, get Mum to help you

Toolbox Tip No 8
Managing Perfectionism

Xavier: Nearly done! Perfectionism is next.

Tris: So, you think that it is possible to be a perfectionist, despite having ADHD?

Xavier: Well, I didn't think so, but after working with Joy and learning more about the traits of perfectionism, I can see why Mum says that sometimes things are OK just being 'good enough'.

One thing I know is when I don't think I'll do well enough, I become too afraid to even try. Sometimes I don't do the tasks at all. I also used to seek reassurance all the time. I still do, but not as much.

Tris: So, perfectionism is not necessarily a good thing then, is it?

Xavier: I suppose there is nothing wrong with wanting high standards and working hard to challenge oneself. However, it is not a good thing when it is taken to a level where it impacts your well-being and leads to frustration, avoidance, worry, and a sense of failure.

According to the Centre for Clinical Intervention, the main feature of perfectionism is the tendency to judge your self-worth largely on your ability to achieve high standards, and involves constantly aiming for extremely high standards, despite experiencing negative consequences of setting such demanding standards, yet continuing with that behaviour, despite the huge cost to you.

Perfectionism is different to the motivation for excellence. It keeps gifted perfectionists from feeling good enough about themselves. It keeps children from taking risks. They become so afraid of failure that they avoid work, play, and new experiences altogether. To meet their high standards, perfectionists tend to engage in a number of perfectionism behaviours (e.g., repeatedly checking work for mistakes), which may serve to maintain perfectionistic beliefs.

People don't often think of children with ADHD as perfectionists. Some children with ADHD appear to race through homework without worrying about the results. They may also appear to have difficulties paying attention to detail and following through on projects or assignments, but some (both boys and girls) are perfectionists. And that can be as hard to manage as other behaviours people usually associate with ADHD.

Perfectionism Can Affect School Performance: One of the areas where perfectionism shows up most often is in expressive writing. Children might get stuck on the first line of a paper and keep working on it until it sounds 'just right' to them. Then they get stuck in the same way on the following sentences. Because of this, they write and rewrite until it's just right. It's tedious and time consuming, and prevents them from completing assignments/ tasks.

Perfectionism Can Create Frustration and Anxiety: The need to do something perfectly can create anxiety as well as frustration. Children may worry in advance about doing well on an upcoming assignment or test, leading to increased anxiety. Since children with ADHD typically have trouble managing their emotions, these feelings may be more intense than for other children. They may also last longer than they might in children who don't have ADHD. Worth noting is that sometimes extreme perfectionism may be more a trait of obsessive compulsive disorder (OCD) than of ADHD. If your child with ADHD is a perfectionist, help put things in perspective by explaining when good is 'good enough'.

"Perfectionism is not the same thing as striving to be our best. Perfectionism is not about healthy achievement and growth; it's a shield".

– Brene Brown

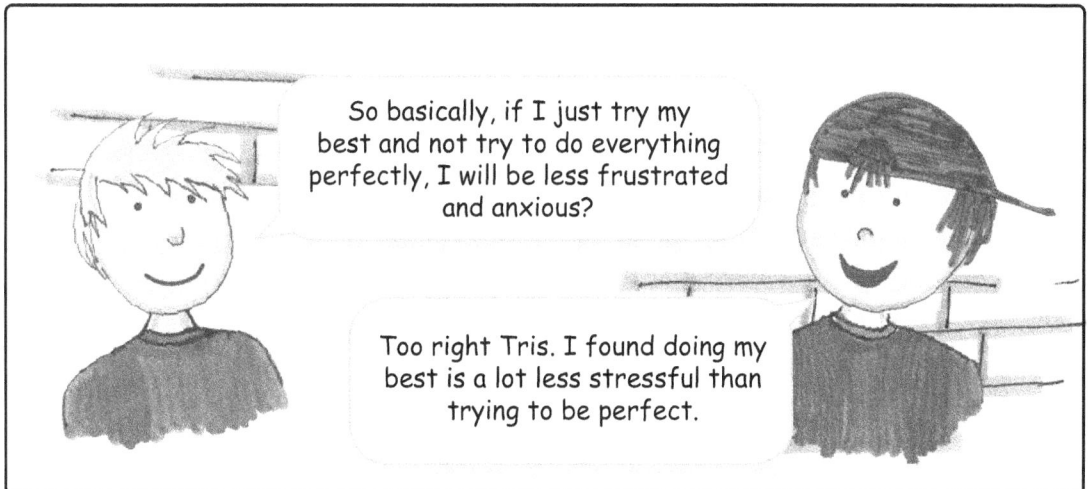

So basically, if I just try my best and not try to do everything perfectly, I will be less frustrated and anxious?

Too right Tris. I found doing my best is a lot less stressful than trying to be perfect.

Toolbox Tip No 9
Building Self-Esteem and Confidence

Xavier: When I got diagnosed at thirteen, I had no confidence at all. I felt inferior to the other kids and always had a sense that I was not good enough as a person. I still struggle with self-esteem, but I am getting better.

Tris: I feel like that at times too. I always compare myself with other kids and then feel that I am not as good or as smart as them. Even when I got that good grade for maths, it was as if a voice inside my head kept on telling me it was just a 'fluke'; that it was never going to happen again.

Xavier: One of the many so called 'cognitive distortions' (thinking traps) that individuals with ADHD engage in is 'comparing'. Let's face it, over-thinking about how someone else is better looking, has more friends, or is more successful than you, is both time-consuming and ineffective. After all, what people present to the outside world is usually an edited version of their reality.

Tris: I do that a lot, but mainly in school – I always feel inferior to the other kids in my class.

Self-esteem usually refers to how we view and think about ourselves and the value that we place on ourselves as a person. If this value is more negative than positive, we run into problems with self-esteem.

Low self-esteem is having a generally negative overall opinion of oneself, judging or evaluating oneself negatively, and placing a general negative value on oneself as a person.

People with low self-esteem usually have deep-seated, negative core beliefs about themselves and the kind of person they are. These beliefs are often taken as facts or truths about their identity, rather than being recognised as opinions they hold about themselves. They might put themselves down, doubt themselves, or blame themselves when things go wrong. They ignore positive qualities and when compliments are given to them, they might brush such comments aside or say that "it was all luck" or "it wasn't that big a deal."

Instead, they might focus on what they didn't do or the mistakes they made. They might also be less likely to stand up for themselves or protect themselves from being bullied, criticised, or abused by partners or family. On the other hand, they can be overly aggressive in their interactions with others.

Educating yourself about your ADHD is the first step to start rebuilding feelings of confidence and personal satisfaction. Like they say, 'knowledge is power'. The more you know about your ADHD, or any other condition for that matter, and how to manage its symptoms, the more confident and in control you feel. The tips that follow may help you discover the 'real person' who may be buried under the extra baggage that comes with having ADHD:

- **Visualise the new you:** Use mental imaging to create a picture of the new you. Having better relationships, getting better grades, volunteering at an organisation that you like or working at a part-time job.

- **Explore your values:** Know what you stand for in life (what makes you who you are).

- **Set reasonable value-based goals:** It's good to have goals and dreams. But be sure to set realistic ones that are in service of your values.

- **Give yourself constructive criticism:** When you don't achieve a goal, don't beat yourself up. Try to understand why you did not achieve it – poor organisation, not realistic, not enough effort, etc. Use perceived failure as an opportunity to learn and grow.

- **Join a peer support group:** Sharing your experiences with others who are dealing with similar problems can give you new strategies and resources.

- **Join 'fun' groups:** Look for groups to join, for example scouts. At school, debating, journalism or drama clubs may interest you. If you like helping others, look into volunteering.

- **Take up a sport or hobby:** Physical hobbies can help you work off pent-up physical or mental energy, and redirect it in constructive ways.

- **Having friends:** It is important that a new friend understands and accepts you as you are. If you start changing just so that someone will accept you, you will have a hard time sorting out your real friends.

- **Dating:** When it comes to dating, girls with ADHD should be especially careful not to use sex as a tool for gaining acceptance from boys. Let your values, rather than your condition, control the decisions you make.

As self-esteem, confidence, and feelings of self-worth grow, they feed off each other – strength leads to strength. As you become more confident and surer of yourself, you will feel less angry and anxious and more proactive in your actions.

Also important to note is that just like people without ADHD, you have a wide variety of intellectual abilities, special talents, and unique interests. People with ADHD have personalities that range from life of the party to wallflowers – just like people without ADHD. People with ADHD range from workaholics to slackers, just like people without ADHD.

So, even though ADHD is a medical condition, when it is well-managed it is not necessarily a handicap in the career world. This means that when you are planning a career, you bring to the job search the same abilities, characteristics, and capabilities as someone without ADHD. More importantly, the career you choose should give you a chance to maximise your strengths, especially your unique ability to look at situations with creativity and tap into your very high energy levels.

You need to know the 'WHO' (who you are), before you can possibly know the 'WHAT' (what you want). If you don't go within! You will go without.

– Neale Walsch

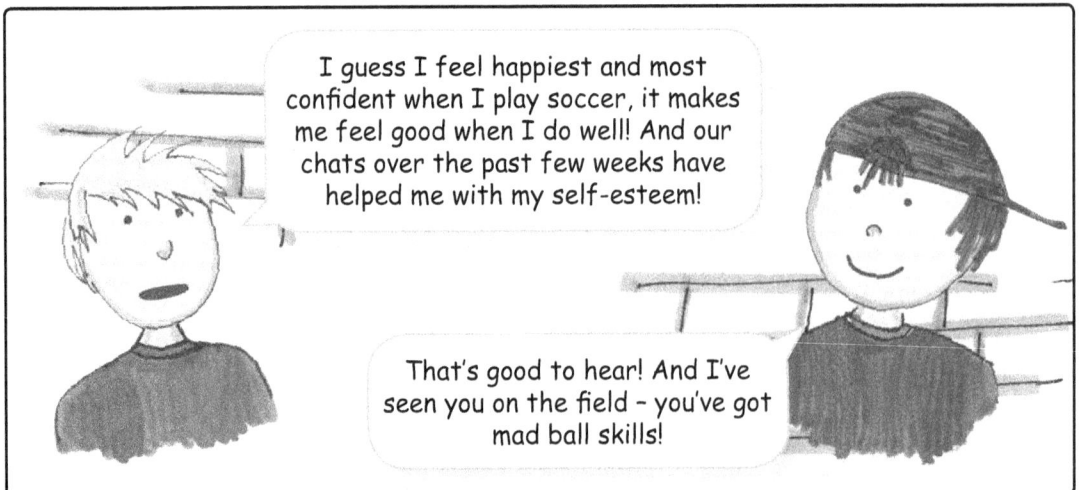

I guess I feel happiest and most confident when I play soccer, it makes me feel good when I do well! And our chats over the past few weeks have helped me with my self-esteem!

That's good to hear! And I've seen you on the field – you've got mad ball skills!

Toolbox Tip No 10
Unhelpful Thinking Styles (Thinking Traps)

Xavier: Remember I told you that Joy taught me about what she calls 'thinking traps' (unhelpful thinking styles)?

Tris: Yeah, I remember like comparing, which I do a lot.

Xavier: Exactly! Well, this is a list of the most common 'thinking traps' that individuals with ADHD engage in, even in the absence of co-existing mood and anxiety disorder.

Individuals who grow up with ADHD (particularly if it has gone undiagnosed) encounter more frequent and frustrating setbacks in life situations — at school, on the job, in social interactions, and with everyday organisation. Because of these setbacks, individuals with ADHD become self-critical and pessimistic. This, in turn, causes them to experience negative emotions, cognitive distortions, and unhealthy self-beliefs. It is common for individuals living with ADHD to think they are at fault when situations don't turn out well, when, in many cases, they are not at fault. They may bring the same pessimism to the future, imagining that tomorrow will go as badly as today.

Unhelpful thinking styles can become an automatic habit, something that happens without our awareness. Constantly and consistently using these styles of thinking can cause a great deal of emotional distress. This information sheet describes a number of 'unhelpful thinking styles'. As you read through them, you might notice some thinking patterns and styles that you use consistently.

Below is a list of common thinking errors in ADHD adapted from Ramsay, Russell, J., & Rostain, Anthony, L. (2015).

- **All-or-nothing thinking:** You view everything as entirely good or entirely bad: If you don't do something perfectly, you've failed.

- **Over-generalisation:** You see a single negative event as part of a pattern: For example, you always forget to hand in your homework.

- **Mind reading:** You think you know what people think about you or something you've done — and it's bad.

- **'Fortune telling':** You are certain that things will turn out badly.

- **Magnification and minimisation:** You exaggerate the significance of minor problems, while trivialising your accomplishments.

- **'Should' statements:** You focus on how things should be, leading to severe self-criticism, as well as feelings of resentment toward others.

- **Personalisation:** You blame yourself for negative events and downplay the responsibility of others.

- **Mental filtering:** You see only the negative aspects of any experience.

- **Emotional reasoning:** You assume that your negative feelings reflect reality: Feeling bad about your job means, "I'm doing badly and will probably get fired."

- **Comparative thinking:** You measure yourself against others and feel inferior, even though the comparison may be unrealistic.

"If you are searching for that one person who will change your life ... take a look in the mirror".

– Unknown

Toolbox Tip No 11
Bullying

Xavier: Although our school has a good policy on bullying, and it doesn't seem to be a problem, bullying is happening in many places – not just in schools. For that reason, I have included some information and tips on bullying.

Tris: I hope that I am not ever going to need it!

Xavier: Hopefully not, but maybe this information can help you to help someone else who is being bullied. Who knows?

Tris: Cool.

Bullying is when a person purposefully hurts others with words or actions. Bullies will pick on their target over and over, and it can be hard to make them stop. Bullying is different from the typical disagreements or conflict that occur between friends or classmates. It is distinct from other forms of aggressive behaviours by encompassing three elements:

- First, bullying occurs between individuals of the same age group. Bullying can take place between youths or between adults.

- Second, the hurtful actions are repeated over time so a pattern of interactions is established between the bullies and a victim. One-off incidents involving hurtful actions between individuals are not examples of bullying behaviour.

- Third, the relationship between the bullies and a victim is characterised by a power imbalance whereby it is difficult for the victim to defend him/herself. Physical strength, popularity and age are factors that characterise power imbalance between the bullies and their victim (Arseneault, L., Bowes, L., and Shakoor, S., 2010).

In summary, bullying is when:

- The person is being hurt, harmed or humiliated with words or behaviour.

- The behaviour is repeated, though it can be a single incident.

- It is being done intentionally.

- The person being hurt has a hard time defending themselves from the behaviour.

- The individuals who are doing it have more power. Power can include such things as being older, being physically bigger or stronger, having more social status, or when a group of students 'gang up' on someone.

Types of Bullying:

Physical	Verbal	Social	Cyber
Hitting	Name calling	Spreading rumours	Sharing embarrassing photos/videos
Kicking	Teasing	Causing embarrassment	Sending hurtful comments/ messages
Pushing	Making hurtful comments	Encouraging others to exclude from group	Impersonating another person online
Tripping	Threats		
Shoving or intimidating			
Damaging or stealing belongings			

Feel free to add your own examples

Adapted from TherapistAid.com

Dealing with Bullies

1. Talk to an Adult / Ask for Advice

Telling and tattling are two different things. When a person tattles, they just want to see someone else get in trouble. Telling, on the other hand, is about helping. If you or someone else is being bullied, reporting it to an adult is telling, not tattling!

List three adults you can talk to about a bully.

1_____

2_____

3_____

2. Don't Show Your Feelings

Bullies like to pick on people who they can control. If a bully realises that they can upset you, they're more likely to keep coming back. By ignoring the bully, you are showing that you don't care. Eventually the bully will probably get bored with trying to bother you.

3. Avoid the Bully and use the 'Buddy System'

Whenever reasonable, simply walk away, or avoid the bully entirely. For example, take a different path to class, or pretend like you didn't hear the bully and keep walking. Buddy up with a friend on the bus, hallways, at recess - wherever the bully is.

4. Be Assertive and Confident

Bullies avoid people who seem confident, or sure of themselves. Even if you don't feel confident, you can pretend by standing tall, responding with a calm and clear voice, and making eye contact. Try practising your confident response before you need it.

5. Respond Neutrally

Bullies quickly grow bored with neutral responses. The key is to seem uninterested in what the bully has to say, without giving a reason to argue. Neutral responses might sound like:

'So?' 'Who cares?' 'Maybe.' 'That's your opinion.'

If bullying happens to you, do not blame yourself. No one deserves to be bullied or put down. Feeling sad, hurt, scared and confused is common. Learning to control these initial reactions can help. Remember to use your breathing as a technique to maintain self-control.

WHAT ABOUT MY FUTURE?

You are the architect of your future. The fact that you are reading this guide and educating yourself about your diagnosis shows that you are reflecting on your strengths and weaknesses and taking steps to prepare yourself for your future. We know that teens with ADHD are at risk for potentially serious problems as they transition into adulthood. We also know that as many as two-thirds of teens with ADHD continue to experience significant symptoms of ADHD in adulthood. In addition, as they become adults, teens with ADHD are at higher risk for difficulties in education, occupation and social relationships. However, these are only risks; they are not guarantees.

With hard work and support, you will be able not only to 'just get by' through school, but to follow your dreams wherever they lead you. Most teens with ADHD become successful, productive adults, and so can you! Continued awareness and treatment is crucial so that you can avoid the risks and meet the goals you set for yourself, whatever they are.

This guide will help you learn different ways to approach every part of your life and to see that you are not alone. Understanding, managing and coping with ADHD requires great determination and perseverance. But with understanding comes acceptance. Acceptance does not mean you are happy with your condition, only that you recognise it for what it is.

As you learn to embrace, rather than fight your ADHD, you may find that what you thought was your ADHD 'negatives' can become the engine that powers your journey to become a source of strength, inspiration and comfort to those feeling stuck or challenged by a difficult obstacle.

"Once I accepted my ADHD, life began to change."

– Xavier

Glossary

ADHD (Attention Deficit Hyperactivity Disorder): A mild to severe neurobiological (brain) condition that is characterised by the inability to focus, concentrate, and pay attention for long periods of time.

ADHD Coach: A person who helps individuals with ADHD manage the challenges that ADHD creates for them and their families.

Behaviour modification: Skills, strategies and techniques that help bring about change and modify the negative behaviours and attitudes that often accompany ADHD.

Co-existing: Conditions that exist together or at the same time.

Counsellor: A professional who works with people to help them understand their feelings and solve their problems.

Diagnosis: Identifying and describing a medical condition.

Empathy: To be in tune with the feelings of others.

Hyperactivity: Excessive amount of activity and energy.

Impulsivity: Acting or speaking without thinking about the consequences.

Inattention: Easily distracted and unable to pay attention or focus.

Low self-esteem: Lack of confidence in one's capabilities.

Multimodal: Treatment that combines more than one method at the same time.

Paediatrician: A doctor who specialises in working with children.

Peer group: people usually of the same age and grade who have things in common.

Peer support group: a group of people with similar problems or challenges who gather to share information and support each other.

Prioritise: To organise and rank activities in order of importance.

Psychiatrist: A doctor who specialises in mental health conditions and prescribes medication accordingly.

Psychologist: A person who studies how people think and behave. Psychologists talk to people about their feelings and help them feel better.

Self-confidence: Trust in one's abilities.

Sibling: Brother or sister.

Side-effects: Ways that medication can affect people negatively.

Stimulant: A class of medication that increases mental activity.

Supplements: Products that help provide you with nutrients your body and brain need to remain in top shape.

Symptom: Characteristics that help to differentiate and name disorders and illnesses.

Therapist: A person who is trained to treat physical or mental health conditions.

Therapy: The process of treating an injury, disease or mental health condition.

Traits: Distinguishing characteristics or qualities, especially of one's personality.

Unhelpful thinking styles: Negative thinking that is damaging to the self and makes change difficult.

Values: Values refer to what is really important to us. They give us insight into who we really are. Values give our life meaning and purpose.

Bibliography

American Psychiatric Association 2013, *Diagnostic and Statistical Manual of Mental Disorders (DSM-5)*, American Psychiatric Association Publishing, Washington, D.C:

Arseneault, L, Bowes, L & Shakoor, S 2010, 'Bullying victimization in youths and mental health problems: "much ado about nothing"?' *Psychological Medicine*, 40, pp 717729 doi:10.1017/S0033291709991383

Ashley, Susan 2005, *The ADD & ADHD Answer Book* Sourcebooks, Inc. Naperville Illinois

Barkley, RA 2000, *Taking Charge of ADHD* The Guilford Press, New York, NY

Barkley RA & Murphy, KR 2006, *Attention deficit hyperactivity disorder: A clinical workbook* 3rd edn, Guilford Publications. New York

Barkley, RA & Murphy, KR 2011, 'The nature of executive function (EF) deficits in daily life activities in adults with ADHD and their relationship to EF tests.' *Journal of Psychopathology and Behavioral Assessment.*

Bernstein, G & Layne, A 2004, 'Separation anxiety and generalized anxiety disorder.' In J Wiener and M Dulcan (eds) *Textbook of Child and Adolescent Psychiatry* 3rd edn, American Psychiatric Publishing, Arlington, VA

Brown, TE 2005, *Attention Deficit Disorder: The unfocused mind in children and adults.* Yale University Press, New Haven

Brown, TE 2016, *ADHD in girls and boys: Is it different?* Understood. org

Brown, TE (ed) 2000, *Attention deficit disorders and comorbidities in children, adolescents and adults.* American Psychiatric Publishing, Inc, Arlington, VA

Centre for Clinical interventions: Perfectionism Behaviours; Psychotherapy Research and Training: <www.cci.health.wa.gov.au>

Chan, E, Ugenia, M, Rappaport, M, Leonard, A & Kemper, K 2003, 'Complementary and Alternative Therapies in Childhood Attention and Hyperactivity Problems.' *Journal of Developmental & Behavioral Pediatrics,* February 2003, vol 24, issue 1, pp 4-8

Dodson, W 2018, *ADHD in Exile: When the Shame of Living with a Disorder Is Worse Than the Disorder Itself.* <www.additudemag.com/slideshows/adhd-and-shame>

Jones, HA, Raggi, VL & Chronis-Tuscano, AM 2006, 'Evidence-based psychosocial treatments for children and adolescents with attention-deficit/hyperactivity disorder', *Clinical Psychology Review*, 26. 486-502. 10.1016/j.cpr.2006.01.002.

Kadesjo, B & Gillberg, C 2001, 'The comorbidity of ADHD in the general population of Swedish school-age children.' *Journal of Child Psychology and Psychiatry* May; 42 (4): 487-92.

Meyer, Harold. *6 Steps to a Thorough ADHD Evaluation*, <www.additudemag.com/download/>

Pelham WE, Burrows-MacLean L, Gnagy EM, Fabiano GA, Coles EK, Wymbs BT, Chacko A, Walker KS, Wymbs F, Garefino A, Hoffman MT, Waxmonsky JG& Waschbusch DA 2014, 'A dose-ranging study of behavioral and pharmacological treatment in social settings for children with ADHD.' *Journal of Abnormal Child Psychology* doi: 10.1007/s10802-013-9843-8

Peterson, BS, Pine, DS, Cohen, P, & Brook, JS 2001, 'Prospective, longitudinal study of tic, obsessive-compulsive, and attention-deficit/hyperactivity disorders in an epidemiological sample.' *Journal of the American Academy of Child and Adolescent Psychiatry*, 40, 685-695.

Price, A 2017, *He's not lazy: empowering your son to believe in himself*, Sterling Publishing Co, New York, NY

Silver, LB 1999, *Dr. Larry's advice to parents of children with ADHD*, Three Rivers Press, New York, NY

Solanto, MV 2011, *Cognitive-Behavioral Treatment of Adult ADHD: Targeting Executive Dysfunction.* Guilford Press, New York, NY

Stallard, P 2005, *A clinician's guide to Think Good – Feel Good: Using CBT with children and young people*, Wiley, Milton, Qld

The Royal Australasian College of Physicians 2009, *Australian Guidelines on Attention Deficit Hyperactivity Disorder,* RACP, Sdney, NSW

Understood team, *ADHD and perfectionism. What you need to know* <www.understood.org>

Young, S & Smith, J 2017, *Helping Children with ADHD: A CBT Guide for Practitioners, Parents and Teachers,* Wiley-Blackwell, Hoboken, NJ

Zeigler, CA, Zeigler, D & Zeigler, A 2003, *A Bird's Eye View of Life with ADD and ADHD: Advice from young survivors.* 2nd edn, Cherish the Children, Cedar Bluff, Alabama

Zeigler Dendy, CA 2011, *Teaching teens with ADD, ADHD & executive functioning deficits: a quick reference guide for teachers and parents.* 2nd edn, Woodbine House, Bethesda, MD

Resources: Useful websites

Additude: http://www.additude.com (a consumer-focused website designed to provide current, information for children and adults with ADHD and other learning difficulties. Resources include; articles, book reviews, webinars, blogs and more.

Attention Deficit Disorder Association (ADDA): http://www.add.org

Behaviour Management: http://www.disciplinehelp.com

Centre for Clinical Intervention: www.cci.health.wa.gov.au

CHADD: http://www.chadd.org – this websites has information sheets, research studies as well as links to other services.

Conduct disorders: http://www.conductdisorders.com – provides resources and information on Oppositional-Defiant Disorder (ODD), Conduct Disorder (CD) and ADHD.

Healthtalk: ADHD http://www2.healthtalk.com/go/adhd

National Centre for Learning Disabilities – http://www.ncld.org

National Institute of Mental Health (NIMH) – http://www.nimh.nih.gov

TherapistAid.com

Understood: www.understood.org

WebMD and ADHD Health Centre – http://www.webmd.com/add-adhd

NOTES

NOTES

NOTES

NOTES

www.ingramcontent.com/pod-product-compliance
Lightning Source LLC
Chambersburg PA
CBHW081157270326
41930CB00014B/3188